DRINKING AND SOBRIETY AMONG THE LAKOTA SIOUX

CONTEMPORARY NATIVE AMERICAN COMMUNITIES
Stepping Stones to the Seventh Generation

Acknowledging the strength and vibrancy of Native American people and nations today, this series examines life in contemporary Native American communities from the point of view of Native concerns and values. Books in the series cover topics that are of cultural and political importance to tribal peoples and that affect their possibilities for survival, in both urban and rural communities.

SERIES EDITORS:

Troy Johnson, American Indian Studies, California State University, Long Beach, Long Beach, CA 90840, trj@csulb.edu

Duane Champagne, Native Nations Law and Policy Center, 292 Haines Hall, Box 951551, University of California, Los Angeles, Los Angeles, CA 90095-1551, champagn@ucla.edu

BOOKS IN THE SERIES

1. *Inuit, Whaling, and Sustainability*, Milton M R Freeman, Ingmar Egede, Lyudmila Bogoslovskaya, Igor G Krupnik, Richard A. Caulfield and Marc G. Stevenson (1999)
2. *Contemporary Native American Political Issues*, edited by Troy Johnson (1999)
3. *Contemporary Native American Cultural Issues*, edited by Duane Champagne (1999)
4. *Modern Tribal Development: Paths to Self Sufficiency and Cultural Integrity in Indian Country*, Dean Howard Smith (2000)
5. *American Indians and the Urban Experience*, edited by Susan Lobo and Kurt Peters (2001)
6. *Medicine Ways: Disease, Health, and Survival among Native Americans*, edited by Clifford Trafzer and Diane Weiner (2001)
7. *Native American Studies in Higher Education: Models for Collaboration between Universities and Indigenous Nations*, edited by Duane Champagne and Jay Stauss (2002)
8. *Spider Woman Walks This Land: Traditional Cultural Properties and the Navajo Nation*, by Kelli Carmean (2002)
9. *Alaska Native Political Leadership and Higher Education: One University, Two Universes*, by Michael Jennings (2004)
10. *Indigenous Intellectual Property Rights: Legal Obstacles and Innovative Solutions*, edited by Mary Riley (2004)
11. *Healing and Mental Health for Native American: Speaking in Red*, edited by Ethan Nebelkopf and Mary Phillips (2004)
12. *Rachel's Children*, by Lois Beardslee (2004)
13. *A Broken Flute: The Native Experience in Books for Children*, edited by Doris Seale and Beverly Slapin (2005)
14. *Indigenous Peoples & the Modern State*, edited by Duane Champagne, Karen Torjesen & Susan Steiner [2005]
15. *Reading Native American Women: Critical/Creative Representations*, edited by Inés Hernández-Ávila (2005)
16. *Native Americans in the School System: Family, Community, and Academic Achievement*, by Carol Ward (2005)
17. *Indigenous Education and Empowerment: International Perspectives*, edited by Ismael Abu-Saad and Duane Champagne (2005)
18. *Cultural Representation in Native America*, edited by Andrew Jolivétte (2006)
19. *Social Change and Cultural Continuity Among Native Nations*, by Duane Champagne (2006)
20. *Drinking and Sobriety among the Lakota Sioux*, by Beatrice Medicine (2006)

DRINKING AND SOBRIETY AMONG THE LAKOTA SIOUX

BEATRICE MEDICINE

ALTAMIRA PRESS
A Division of Rowman & Littlefield Publishers, Inc.
Lanham • New York • Toronto • Plymouth, UK

ALTAMIRA PRESS
A division of Rowman & Littlefield Publishers, Inc.
A wholly owned subsidiary of The Rowman & Littlefield Publishing Group, Inc.
4501 Forbes Boulevard, Suite 200, Lanham, MD 20706
www.altamirapress.com

Estover Road, Plymouth PL6 7PY, United Kingdom

British Library Cataloguing in Publication Information Available

Library of Congress Cataloging-in-Publication Data

Medicine, Beatrice.
  Drinking and sobriety among the Lakota Sioux / Beatrice Medicine.
    p. cm. — (Contemporary Native American communities : stepping stones to the
seventh generation)
  Includes bibliographical references and index.
  ISBN-13: 978-0-7591-0570-6 (cloth : alk. paper)
  ISBN-10: 0-7591-0570-7 (cloth : alk. paper)
  ISBN-13: 978-0-7591-0571-3 (pbk. : alk. paper)
  ISBN-10: 0-7591-0571-5 (pbk. : alk. paper)
  1. Dakota Indians—Alcohol use. 2. Drinking of alcoholic beverages—Great Plains.
3. Alcoholism—Great Plains—Treatment. 4. Alcoholism—Great Plains—Prevention.
I. Title.

  E99.D1M52 2006
  362.292'089975243—dc22

                                                              2006018523

Printed in the United States of America

∞™ The paper used in this publication meets the minimum requirements of American
National Standard for Information Sciences—Permanence of Paper for Printed Library
Materials, ANSI/NISO Z39.48-1992.

CONTENTS

Introduction

THIS INVESTIGATION EXTENDS my earlier study (Medicine 1969) on changes in family structure associated with a perceived increase in the use of alcohol, and it departs from previous studies of Indian alcoholism in important ways. Initially, it utilized an indigenous perspective building upon ethnotheories and ethnomethodologies derived from the Lakota Sioux. Native articulations regarding why people choose to drink, how they were socialized to drinking, and the rationale for drunken behavior were used as data-gathering guides. Moreover, as the subjects of this investigation were interviewed—many in their native language—new ethnolinguistic categories of drinking and sober states were developed. This approach has been used also in studies dealing with American Indian drinking among Navajo males (Topper 1980, 1981). Native categories as they reflect perceptions of self and worldview are newer approaches to treatment in mental health and in social disorders—alcohol abuse being a predominant one among Indian groups.

This is a unique study of the seldom-explored topic of activating indigenous ways to sobriety. Previous studies have concentrated upon drinking styles of aboriginal populations. This investigation looks at an indigenous culture, the Lakota, through the experiences of members of that native society. It deals with the subject of alcohol consumption and the means of attaining sobriety as seen through the experiences of Lakota alcoholics. The strategies that these Lakotas developed to attain a new sober lifestyle have the potential to help others attain sobriety.

Alcohol use has preoccupied ethnographers (Barnouw 1950; Underhill 1938, 1946; Wallace 1959) and historians (Johnson 1917; Saum 1965;

Stein 1974; Winkler 1968) for many years, with differential reporting upon various tribal groups deriving from several theoretical viewpoints. The amount of research on alcohol use has increased since the late 1960s, and the topic remains the focus of many social scientists, including psychologists (Mohatt 1972; McClelland et al. 1972), sociologists (Kunitz 1977), psychiatrists (Westermeyer 1972, 1974), and of course, anthropologists (Leland 1976, 1978, 1979, 1980; Lurie 1971, 1972; Topper 1976, 1980). Other persons in the helping professions—nurses, doctors, and social workers—have not initiated extensive research but have used some of the results in proposed treatments. Social science interest in the subject is apparent in the statistics dealing with the horrendous effects of alcohol on the lives of Indian people in most areas of native North America. Not only does alcohol consumption have deleterious effects upon individual lives, but also alcohol-related behaviors—which are basic to increased crime, suicide, and homicide rates—have devastated Indian communities. Equally damaging to the quality of life among Indian groups are the alcohol-induced instances of child, spouse, and parent abuse and other social disorders. These dismal facts are often recited as a litany of social problems that beset American Indians and Alaska Natives. Moreover, such data have served as the basis for funding requests and applied programs to ameliorate the salient social problem in these societies. That the myriad and sometimes contradictory studies may have been used as a means of obtaining finances in the name of those powerless peoples is not lost on them (V. Deloria 1969; Maynard 1974). Moreover, the discontent with these studies has led to Tribal Councils, the National Congress of American Indians, and other indigenous groups attempting to gain power in the situation through the establishment of tribal Institutional Review Boards (IRBs) and other mechanisms to attempt to control the type and scope of research imposed upon them.

Use of the terms "American Indian" and, more recently, "Native American" has led to great misinterpretation in the literature of alcoholism resulting from studies of this culturally heterogeneous population. Information yielded by the investigation of one tribal group has been transposed to another, sometimes totally unrelated, cultural or linguistic group or has not allowed for great intergroup variation (Waldram 2004). This has not allowed for stringent theory building or effective application.

As superimposed policies and institutional procedures regarding tribal peoples of North America have changed, so have the names that were applied to these groups. Indian, American Indian, Red Indian, Amerindian, Indian-American and, more recently, Native American have been used.[1] It is now somewhat unfashionable and nonpolitic to use Native American. Groups such as Native Hawaiians, Samoans, Pacific Islanders, and others have also been assigned this gloss in recent years. Indeed, some conservative Caucasian pundits have adopted "Native American" in its truest linguistic sense—born in America—in their continuing vilification of America's immigrant (and by implication, immigrant of color) population. Thus, it appears that American Indian as a total designation is in vogue again. However, it has been, and still is, apparent that each tribe has a unique identification that it wishes preserved. Each distinctive name often derives from the native linguistic classification for themselves. Each tribal aggregate has a distinctive name. This self-ascribed name may have been overshadowed by another appellation. For example, the Chippewa name for the Lakota was *Nadoweisiw-eg*, which was corrupted into "Sioux" by the French. The "Sioux," who are the subject of this study, call themselves Lakota, Dakota, or Nakota, which is reflective of the particular dialects of the branch of the Siouan language family that they speak. The federal government's designative nomenclature for these people is "Sioux." They also identify themselves by the present geographical reservation assigned to them. Thus, designations of "Standing Rock Sioux" or "Pine Ridge Sioux" are common. This identification is not onerous to most Sioux persons. *Lakota* means humans or "the allies." Lakota people from Standing Rock reservation in North and South Dakota are the focus of this investigation.

Studies on "Indian drinking" have tended to obscure unique tribal characteristics. But researchers seem caught in an untenable situation. While many have stressed the unique, tribal-specific approach, most have given indications of a Pan-tribal quality to the investigations. As a result, policy makers, helping professionals (such as social workers, alcoholism counselors, medical personnel, and missionaries), and others have often been unable to assess the efficacy of the researchers' efforts. Various interpretations of Indian drinking have seemingly contributed to the lack of effective treatments. Whatever the original purpose of research on alcohol use among these native peoples, its underlying purpose tends to be to develop rehabilitative treatments.

The state of knowledge regarding Indian alcoholism is also influenced by a wide variety of theoretical viewpoints. The volume of published data tends to focus on such topics as acculturation (Graves 1967; Hamer 1965; Hornby and Dana 1984; MacGregor 1945), social problems (Coffey 1966; Dozier 1966; Levy and Kunitz 1971a), urbanization (Ablon 1964, 1965, 1971; Graves 1971; Price 1968), and mental health issues (Barter and Barter 1974; Beiser 1974).

Throughout the history of alcoholism studies, the diversity of theories and the unique natures of the ethnographic enclaves of American Indians led to site-specific approaches to data collection, thereby limiting generalization, refinement, and application. Thus, a coherent body of theoretical interpretations to deal with levels of adaptive processes for natives of North America has not been forthcoming. That is, the basic premise that cultures were holistic, well integrated, and unique—a tenant of the anthropological enterprise—seldom yielded a sophisticated overarching explanation of alcohol consumption that had cross-tribal relevance. Clarification of the nexus of the functioning native culture within the larger social domain in which alcohol use was embedded seemed essential. In examining alcohol studies, aspects of colonization and subordination of native societies—indeed, the very aspect of power and exploitation—were seldom considered.

Acculturational stress on the part of the indigenous peoples has been a salient feature in explaining alcohol addiction. Boyer (1964) indicates a common theme when she suggests that the destruction of men's roles as hunter and warrior among the Apache, with resulting idleness, fostered a propensity to drinking alcohol. This theme is also stressed for the Lakota by such writers as Hurt and Brown (1965), Maynard (1969), Mohatt (1972), and Whittaker (1963, 1966). "Deculturation" by natives has been used as an explanatory device for "problems" other than alcohol. As a social process it is a diffuse and all-encompassing concept that needs further refinement as an explanatory device.

Moreover, the view that maladjustment and pathology predominated in these alcohol-ridden societies was the prominent characteristic of most of these studies. Such maladjustments were seen as a result of social deprivation (Dozier 1966; Littman 1970; Stewart 1964). A deficit model comes into focus beginning in the 1960s. Conditions, such as unemployment, poor health, improper diet, low income, inadequate housing, inferior education, and lack of good self-image were all seen as dysfunctional and as fostering excessive use of alcohol (Ablon 1965; Hamer 1965; Hurt 1961; Kemnitzer 1972; Kuttner and Lorincz 1970; Maynard and Twiss 1970; Price 1975; Whittaker 1963, 1966). Maladjustive features of Indian life, in general, were held to account for alcohol use and abuse. Many research reports did not specify amount of deprivation and level of alcohol consumption—nor was cultural deprivation defined in native terms.

Again, few of the published accounts have examined the ethnohistorical backgrounds of the introduction of alcoholic beverages into these tribal groups. Unfortunately, the duration of observation and interaction for many of these investigations was very short. Some did not weigh all sociological, cultural, and psychological variables in which individual behavior is embedded. Others presented a very superficial treatment of a complex, multifaceted situation. It is noteworthy that one of these investigations (Whittaker 1961) was initiated by native peoples themselves. Seldom, however, were indigenous theories or interpretations incorporated into research designs.

My concern with issues of dissonances of individual behavior in my birth culture, the Lakota Sioux, has influenced my involvement in mental health, identity concerns, and finally in a long-term examination of alcohol use, abuse, and ultimately in the native control mechanisms developed by some imbibers. The goal of this study is to present data that add to the understanding of the relationship between alcohol consumption, addiction, and culture from the viewpoint of a participant in that culture. As noted above, this approach is relatively new in ethnographic reporting, for it deals with elements of affect and disengagement—not only among the members of the anthropological discipline but also among the professions dedicated to the prevention of alcohol abuse—social workers, public health officials, and other practitioners concerned with the control of alcohol. Indigenous perspectives are often considered "subjective."

The approach from an indigenous perspective has its adherents. Heath (1981), reviewing Bob Thomas's discussion, notes:

> A very different point of view is expressed by an anthropologist who is also an American Indian. His overview of the history of drinking and its sequel among various populations is engaging, in large part, because it is so highly personal. Readers who have some familiarity with the wide range of ethnographic and historical data on the subject may take issue with some of Thomas's generalizations, but it seems valuable to have such a sensitive, "insider's view" to complement more scholarly accounts. (3)

This "insider's view" gained currency in the 1980s with researchers and funding agencies and led to new treatment strategies, because as Everett (1980), writing after experience with the White Mountain Apaches, states: "it is our contention that [previous] theories and research methodologies have contributed little to an understanding of the meanings of Native American drinking practices and even less to the development of effective treatment and prevention strategies, for Indian alcoholism and problem drinking" (xvii). The fact that previous research on alcohol use and abuse among American Indian groups has seldom resulted in suggestions for applicability and generalizability has been basic to my doing this study.

The Method

The collection of the data included direct observation, beginning with an interpretation of changes in Lakota family structure in 1969. Research continued to 1979 and persisted from durations of four weeks to nine months using participant observation throughout the entire study. Periodic visits to the Standing Rock reservation followed. The times of visits did not coincide with the summer months, as is usual among researchers in American Indian and Alaska Native communities. Instead visits spanned entire years in all seasons. Case studies were collected from thirty-six males and ten female alcoholics, who had achieved some semblance of sobriety. These individuals, who were well known in the communities, provided data that were then coalesced into composite case studies. Case studies seemed necessary, for in this face-to-face society the true identity of the individuals was easily ascertained. Though confidentiality has not been a concern for many researchers and has been the source of much discontent for American Indians, it was felt to be a protective device for the anonymity of the individuals.

Continuous ethnographic observations began in earnest in 1969 to determine the extent and direction of alcohol use. Besides the standard observational techniques utilized by anthropologists, I did informal interviews. However, I hesitate to state that I was a true "participant observer." Owing to family constraints and expectations of the communities on the reservation, I was unable, and did not wish to, participate in drinking events. Concentration upon those individuals who had consciously attempted to "quit drinking" was begun in 1976, when I returned home for six months. Periodic visits continued until 1979.

A sharpening of research focus was decided upon after noting that, beginning in approximately 1971, there were several males and females who had been heavy drinkers but who were "trying to quit." I examined the literature regarding sobriety studies for American Indians or Alaska Natives. There were none. Was the stereotype of the "drunken Indian" so pervasive as to preclude attempts at sobriety from purview? It seemed that there was an advent of a stable period in the drinking pattern observed on the reservations in Sioux country. The entire process of seeking a sober state as a way of life needed documentation and explanation.

During the 1960s and onward, alcohol control programs proliferated on reservations throughout North America. The efficacy of concentrating on sobriety maintenance was apparent after I served as a consultant with numerous Tribal Alcohol Programs, at various conferences sponsored by churches, and with private organizations such as the Association of American Indian Affairs. Governmental agencies, such as the National Institute of Mental Health (in the Health and Human Services Administration) and the National Institute of Drug Abuse, as well as private consulting firms, have concentrated upon alcohol abuse by American Indians. Interest in "Indian alcoholism" was at an all-time peak. Studies on Indian drinking styles proliferated (Everett 1970; Everett, Waddell, and Heath 1976; Waddell and Everett 1980).

Though I sat through many conferences dealing with prevention, I was unable to find any significant information on coping with and conquering alcohol abuse. The dynamics of nondrinking were absent. It seemed imperative to examine sobriety if one were committed to the positive aspects of research in an area often seen by Indians and others as one fraught with dangers and disappointments.

The dimensions of alcoholism among Indians are multiple, complex, and far-reaching and must be carefully explicated in any research endeavor. The pervasive implication that alcoholism is the outstanding "problem" of American Indians often leads the investigation into mere reiterations of drinking styles of different tribes. Orientation for change in behavior is often absent. Yet, if the aim of anthropological research is toward generalizability and astute cross-cultural comparisons, one cannot dismiss all the previous studies on "Indian drinking." One must selectively assess and utilize those observations and data from other investigators to illuminate drinking patterns in the present time. In addition, to effectively consider prevention programs, one must search for commonalities across tribal groups. This is increasingly critical as more American Indians and Alaska Natives become urbanized, separated from their ancestral homes. Intertribal marriages and other demographic factors need to be taken into account. I feel that one must go beyond strictly "ethnographic present" data to appreciate cultural change and its manifestations in the life-way of any tribal group as they live today.

Requests for remedial advice are endemic in this type of research. There is a strong factor in the commonly held view by some members of the dominant society that Indian people "should be helping their own people." Though numerous theories have been applied to the drinking habits and subsequent behavior of any tribal group, no simple, yet cogent, explanation has been forthcoming. The reasons for Indians imbibing alcohol are tied to sociocultural backgrounds, economic factors, and status considerations. Alcoholism is an effect of these and other pertinent variables. Understanding and acknowledging the patterned behavior of Indian drinking is of concern, not only to social scientists but also to policy makers in the administered human relationship arena, which characterizes most of contemporary American Indian life. More importantly, an interest in alcohol abuse is increasingly being evidenced by the native peoples themselves. The issue of excessive alcohol use and its subsequent effects in Indian communities must be a priority in the present concern for native self-determination. Self-determination in the selection of a sober state by certain Lakota individuals offers evidences of coping strategies on an individual level.

My decision to include pertinent data from other studies on different tribes has been carefully considered to make native readers aware of social forces that have similarly affected all native peoples in North America. The idiosyncratically unique ethnohistorical account of Lakota Sioux alcohol use can be replicated for other tribes and might give understanding of alcohol addiction. Such cultural nuances as changing sex roles, child training attitudes, and contemporary ethos are factors in a combined ethnohistorical analysis, with a particularistic approach centering upon disruptive behavior resulting from abuse of alcohol.

Conducting this research has not been easy. It has been an extremely painful process. Dependency and despondency are salient features that have been attributed to the American Indian people under consideration (Blakeslee 1955; MacGregor 1945; White 1970). Alcohol and its debilitating effects have been disastrous in many instances. The present study of the ways to sobriety among the Lakota Sioux people might yield new interpretations of coping strategies that may ultimately be beneficial to them.

The objectivity often thought to be inherent in the scientific method is essential to a study of this nature. Too often, persons who are part of the people they research are accused of subjectivity. It is also for this reason that I have selectively chosen studies by others who have investigated alcoholism among the Lakota Sioux and used them to extend my own observations. It might be charged that aspects of new "ethnomethodology" highlight issues of subjectivity in analysis and interpretation. It should be understood, however, that many "hunches" and formulations, derived from my participation in the cultural groups that form the focus of this study, are offered as new insights into what characterizes and directs many lives of the Lakota Sioux in present-day society.

Recent investigations of Indian drinking patterns have indicated the value of culture-specific information about the use of alcohol. Indeed, Waddell and Everett (1980), after years of research among Southwestern

Indian groups, indicate: "Our collective effort has been to point out that there are culture-specific realities and cultural bodies of knowledge about alcohol and its use and abuse that are sufficiently different so that rehabilitative and educational programs must not ignore them" (225). The writer does not wish to enter into the anthropological concern with reflexivity in theory and method. However, it is possible to assess previous studies objectively and to present more data in such a way as to present new insight into the dynamics of alcohol use. Nonetheless, it has been possible to combine ethnohistorical, bicultural, and social-anthropological concerns with a strong emphasis on cognitive approaches to explain alcohol use within one tribe of the northern plains—the Lakota Sioux.

Most of the studies dealing with alcohol use among this group of Siouan speakers concentrate upon a synchronic approach that does not take into account historical development (Blakeslee 1955; Hurt and Brown 1965; Kemnitzer 1972). A diachronic approach to the subject of alcohol use would seem to be a more valuable endeavor. Levy and Kunitz (1974) have compared Hopi, Navajo, and White Mountain Apache in a valuable methodological study. Because it has not been attempted for the Lakota and other Siouan populations, a thoroughgoing examination of the ethnohistorical foundation of liquor introduction and its subsequent use will be a primary focus in this study. Added to this, a social-ecological model (Trimble and Medicine 1976) was selected from among a variety of theoretical approaches used to study alcohol use among the Lakota. This will be explicated further in the section on sobriety. In essence, an ecologically based analysis is productive.

Kunitz (1977) states: "The prevalence, significance, and causes of such phenomena as drinking, suicide, homicide, and accidents, for example, may differ from one tribe to another in consistent ways depending upon ecological adaptation, social organization, and personality structure" (402). By carefully examining the introduction of alcohol into the western Sioux or Teton groups, an emerging ethic of sobriety will be highlighted. The bulk of the published data on alcohol studies among these groups has centered upon Pine Ridge, while other material has been drawn from the Rosebud and Cheyenne River reservations. These ethnic enclaves are within the domain of the Lakota-speaking groups. The Standing Rock Reservation, however, had the distinction of being the first tribe to commission a study on alcohol use (Whittaker 1962, 1963). My study continues the concern for the use and abuse of alcohol, using that reservation as a social system for analysis.

Note

1. "Whites" refers to Euro-Americans and is used as an ethnic marker for these diverse groups by all American Indians. In this study, it is used as a referent to European immigrants. *Washichu* is a widely accepted Siouan term for Europeans.

After numerous hearings held during 1979 and early 1980 throughout the country, the Office of Indian Education and the Department of Health, Education and Welfare ventured forth with still another definition of an Indian. This will not vitiate the definition of the Bureau of Indian Affairs, which defines an Indian as one-fourth Indian blood and living on trust lands, to be eligible for certain of its programs. The American Indian Policy Review Commission's *Final Report*, submitted to Congress on May 17, 1977, in a section entitled "Who Is an Indian?" indicates:

> The Federal Government, State governments, and the Census Bureau all have different criteria for defining "Indians" for statistical purposes, and even Federal criteria are not consistent among Federal agencies. For example, a State desiring financial aid to assist Indian education receives that aid only for the number of people with one-quarter or more Indian blood. For preference in hiring, enrollment records from a federally recognized tribe are required. Under regulations on law and order, anyone "of Indian descent" is counted an Indian.
>
> If federal criteria are inconsistent, state guidelines for deciding who is or is not Indian are even more chaotic. In the course of preparing its report, the commission contacted several states with large Indian populations to determine their criteria. Two states accept the Indian's own determination. Four accept individuals as Indians if they were "recognized in the community" as Native Americans. Five use residence on a reservation as a criterion. One requires one-quarter Indian blood and still another used the Census Bureau definition that Indians are those who say they are.
>
> If simply defining who is an Indian presents problems, compiling other vital statistics about Indians and Indian affairs presents almost insurmountable obstacles. (1977, 89)

"All Indians Are Drunks"
A Pervasive Myth

1

To show the extent of alcohol use among native groups and to understand the scope of the "problem" of alcohol consumption, it is necessary to examine ethnographic data. The term "alcohol," as it is used in reference to American Indians of all tribes, is an exceedingly value-laden and emotion-evoking one. It is historically wedded to the image of drunken native savages murdering and marauding whites on the expanding western frontiers. It is, at present, equally strong in creating the widespread image of the drunken Indian. This descriptive gloss is commonly used in any area where natives of any tribal affiliation reside. It is an all-encompassing and convenient stereotype for all natives—American Indians and Alaska Natives.

The image of the drunken Indian also extends to urban areas where North American Indians increasingly reside and where they are often seen as transitory nomads. Fear of drunken, lewd, and licentious natives living in the vast sociological unknown of reserves and reservations is a predominant theme in Indian-white relationships (Bennett 1969; Braroe 1975; Schusky 1975). Varying degrees of negativity are evident in the association of Indians with alcohol.

Given this prevalent stereotyping, the pattern of alcohol consumption in indigenous societies—past and present—is indeed a delicate issue to confront. Frequently, one is caught in the mesh of conflicting data about alcohol consumption among these aboriginal peoples. The information for most tribes is confounded by scientific and pseudoscientific attempts to assess the native consumption of alcoholic beverages. There were, and are, some tribal societies that presented, and still exhibit, various levels of

1

1

alcohol production. Consumption patterns varied, with resultant behavior modification that ranged, even as it does in the present day, from complete abstinence to active involvement in altered, and in some cases, bizarre and aberrant, behaviors. Fragmentary observations, postulates, theories, and conjectures about American natives abound in the literature dealing with the nature, function, and use of alcohol.

American Indians are alleged to be especially vulnerable to alcohol, to show uncontrolled and deviant behavior when drunk, and to have a tendency to become alcoholics. Scientific evidence to date has not conclusively established whether some human populations are more prone to alcoholism than others. Some studies make this suggestion (Dyck 1986; Fenna et al. 1971; Hanna 1976). As far as the American Indians are concerned, no data indicates any special constitutional factor that gives a biological basis to such prevalent views on native drinking behaviors (Bennion and Li 1976).

In general, the production of alcoholic beverages is tied to such obvious variables as the availability of resources to allow for its production. Thus, the interdependency of raw materials, knowledge of brewing techniques, and patterns of consumption are variables in the total picture of each tribe's use of alcohol. More significantly, there appear to be several "givens" in the sociocultural level of the different social groupings (tribes) of native peoples that allowed or limited the manufacture of alcohol. It is commonly assumed that cereal grains used in the distilling of inebriating beverages were strictly limited to those tribes practicing horticulture. However, many tribes who utilized semi- or fully developed horticulture systems did not manufacture alcoholic spirits. On the other hand, there is evidence that some native groups brewed intoxicants from vegetable materials they gathered. Prudence and extreme caution are needed in the presentation of historical and ethnological data relating the use of alcohol both in the past and in present times.

MacAndrew and Edgerton (1969) write, "Except for a few southwestern tribes, the North American Indians had no alcoholic beverages prior to the coming of the white man" (100). Before European contact, the New World was not entirely without alcohol. Alcoholic beverages were widespread in South America, throughout the Circum-Caribbean region, and in Mesoamerica. In Mexico, for example, the Indians had developed alcoholic beverages primarily from maize (Driver 1961). Wild plums, pineapple, and sarsaparilla roots were also used in Mexico. After the Conquest, brandy, mezcal, and tequila were distilled refinements of indigenous liquors (Driver 1955). Such items as saguaro and pitahaya cacti and mesquite were also used. Maize beer manufacture consisted of three techniques: grains chewed to facilitate fermentation, sprouted maize grains, and the utilization of stalks. Within the last hundred years, sprouted-corn beer manufacture spread northward to the San Carlos, Mescalero, Lipan, and Chiricahua Apaches, where it is known as *tiswin* and *tulapai*.

Ritualized and secular drinking was common in the southwestern United States, where the Yumans and Apache drank informally and in a ritual context. Secular drinking of these southwestern groups, however, was infrequent and apparently peaceable in character (Curley 1967; Lindquist 1923). Imbibing among the Pima and Papago was restricted to a peaceable annual ceremony. The Tohono O'odham (formerly Papago) of Arizona ceremonially drank the fermented fruit of the saguaro cactus. After a fermentation period of four nights, the "Keeper of the Smoke" directed singing, dancing, and speech making. Intoxication was believed to bring rain and continued well-being (Joseph, Spicer, and Chesky 1945). It is remotely possible that some tribes in the American Southeast (Virginia and Carolinas) produced a persimmon wine (Driver 1961). The manufacture, if it was indigenous, did not spread to neighboring tribes, for the rest of the Indians of the eastern seaboard and the Southeast did not manufacture alcohol. One must, at least, acknowledge the "black drink." Adair (1930) notes:

> The celebrated "black drink," general among the Southern Indians, a decoction of the leaves and tender tops and shoots of the *cassine* shrub of the holly family. The drink reported caused a sweating which was supposed to purify, physically and morally. The caffeine in the plant produced stimulation and a strong infusion was a narcotic, used as such by the conjurers to evoke ecstasies. No one is allowed to drink in council unless he has proved himself a brave warrior. (49)

In this context, the "black drink" can hardly be called an intoxicant. It seems to parallel the use of peyote as a slight hallucinogen.

MacAndrew and Edgerton (1969) succinctly summarize the aboriginal state when they write about the absence of alcohol:

> So, too, were the rest of the Indians of North America, for outside the Southwest, the Indians of what is now the United States and Canada had no alcoholic beverages before the coming of the white man. Why alcohol did not spread farther north from Mexico is a puzzling but unanswerable question. It was cherished in Mexico and it later became sought all over North America. Yet the fact remains that the vast majority of these North American Indians, although they possessed many wild and cultivated plants

> suitable for fermentation, had not produced alcoholic beverages prior to the period of European contact. Thus, when the first Europeans set foot upon the northeastern coast of this continent, upon the "New Found Land," they introduced their "ardent spirits" to an unknowing population. (109–10)

The importance of this summary is that it points to the introduction of intoxicants with no modeling or propriety of behavior in a learning context.

MacAndrew and Edgerton (1969) present the most cogent analysis of the introduction of alcoholic beverages to non-Western (formerly called "primitive") peoples around the world, and make a strong case for cultural differences in the display of drunken comportment. They document "drunken Indian behavior" as being learned from the behavior of trappers, traders, and other peripheral members of colonial and frontier society. Observing these models, the "unknowing population" soon learned to imbibe, enjoy, and abuse alcoholic beverages. Therein began a great social upheaval in indigenous societies. Drunkenness has now attained epidemic proportions, and associated social problems abound in native enclaves, whether on reservations or in urban areas. Studies on Indian alcoholism have burgeoned. Theories of cultural deprivation (Dozier 1966); dependency (Hamer 1969); economic inequities (Boyer 1964; Graves 1967; Slater and Albrecht 1972; Useem and Eicher 1970); acculturation stress (Graves 1971; Hamer 1965; Littman 1970; Mohatt 1972); and social disorganization (Honigmann 1965; Weaver and Gartell 1974) dominate the literature of drinking in many tribes. Other research orientations have focused upon such psychological variables as escape from reality (Ablon 1971; Dyer 1969), marginality (Bynam 1972), pathologies (Everett 1970; Levy and Kunitz 1971b), and anxiety reduction (Bacon, Barry, and Child 1965; Ferguson 1968; Honigmann and Honigmann 1945; Lemert 1954). As can be seen by the categorization of possible causal effects for excessive use of alcohol in the native societies, most of the proposed explanations could be evaluated as being within the larger context of culture change.

Some studies have viewed intense alcohol use as a coping mechanism (Honigmann and Honigmann 1970; Jilek-Aall 1974; Maynard 1969). The functional dimensions of alcohol have also been shown in some studies of non-Western drinking habits (Bunzel 1940; Devereux 1948; Honigmann and Honigmann 1945; Mandelbaum 1965). Distinctive and novel approaches have not been lacking in the anthropological literature. Some indicate that drinking fosters social solidarity (Lemert 1954, 1967; Waddell 1975). Still others view the drinking process as validating Indian identity in a variety of ways. Besides serving as boundary-maintaining mechanisms, these studies deal with adjustment processes and are tied to a developmental cycle (Ablon 1964; Lurie 1971; Robbins 1973). The theoretical base and the subsequent interpretations seldom result in a discrete explanation of Indian drinking or yield a generalization that crosses tribal boundaries. Generally, such notions as anomie (Curlee 1969; Levy 1965; and others) or the more frequently invoked "release of aggression" (Boyer 1964; Lemert 1958; Rohner and Rohner 1970; Weaver and Gartell 1974) attempt to account for the drunken behavior and motivational patterns of Indian people, usually males, in states of inebriation. These interpretations have simply obscured the complex social contexts of Indian life and the manifestations of drinking and drunkenness.

Various analyses of alcohol use and attendant social ills abound in the current social science literature. These reports project the implicit idea that tribes have similar problems, and thus, the etiology of alcoholism is the same. Interpretations derived from one study are often applied across tribal boundaries and time periods. The response to this research reflects the prevalent and firmly held belief by the dominant society that there is such a monolithic social and biological entity as the "American Indian." Although this belief itself is a myth, it has had great impact upon the nature of studies and, more crucially, the application of the studies in policy making and ameliorative aspects for all American Indians. The diversity represented by approximately three hundred viable tribes remains a factor for consideration.

Many reports of research on Indian drinking have been quite fragmentary and tentative in approach and design. Many have resulted from studies undertaken for extremely short periods of time. Many have been seen as adjuncts to research on other topics. Some have produced in a retrospective fashion. Most have seen liquor as a salient and enduring "problem" of Indian adjustment to an item introduced in their lives. The "problem" orientation has superseded most other approaches. Essentially, a response to problem alleviation has been implicit. It is not uncommon for assumptions to be made that investigations of the Mescalero Apache (Curley 1967) are relevant to the Forest Potawatomi (Hamer 1965). An Athapaskan-speaking group of hunter and gatherers in the Southwest may be compared to an Algonkian-speaking group in the Woodlands culture area. However, tribal differences do not negate the possibility that some data in alcoholism studies are transferable. For example the Apache materials might have some implications for a Lakota Sioux analysis. American Indian alcohol studies have suffered from lack of critical cross-cultural comparisons. Studies began to appear in the 1970s that addressed this lack (Levy and Kunitz 1971b; Marshall 1979; Waddell and Everett 1980). A newer viewpoint seemed to emerge. Levy and Kunitz (1974) indicate:

> In the case of Indian drinking, however, we think that much of the behavior is learned; this is cultural, and this in turn is largely determined by the ecological adaptation of the tribe in question. We maintain that drinking behavior is mainly a reflection of traditional forms of social organization and cultural values instead of a reflection of social disorganization. (24)

This seems a decided move away from the biological determinist point of view that has been so common among lay people and earlier writers. Waddell and Everett (1980) concentrated on four tribes—Papago, Taos Pueblo, Navajo, and White Mountain Apache—of the Greater Southwest, providing comparative data. They write:

> In acknowledging all of this [seeing Indians as marginalized peoples], it would be sheer delusion to suppose that indigenous societies, in their coping strategies, have not maintained continuity with past traditions. In spite of the credibility of there being a "generalized Indian" or a generalized social margin shared with non-Indians, it still means something to be a Papago, a Tiwa, a Navajo, an Apache. It is not only true in a cultural sense but in terms of more particularistic local histories relative to each other and to outsiders. Not all Papagos, Tiwa, Navajos, or Apaches are equally influenced by whatever has been continuous in their separate traditions but there *are* separate traditions and it seems most necessary to consider differential responses to alcohol in light of their different histories. (xxix)

If indeed, we are concerned with the uniqueness of cultures and the adaptations to cultural change that is evidenced by tribal peoples, one must then examine the ethnohistorical features of a native group. Generalizations may become more significant and treatment modalities more effective if controlled comparisons emerge from disparate studies.

Hunting societies may indicate similar adaptations to alcohol. Aboriginally, the Mescalero Apache had a band type of social organization with a hunting and gathering economy. They have made a similar adaptation to a superimposed cultural system as the Lakota. They engage in a cattle-raising economy with a strong dependence upon governmental supply of unskilled jobs as a source of livelihood. The Mescalero Apache exhibit a high incidence of drinking and drunkenness in a pattern that Curley describes as "blitz" drinking. "Blitz" or "binge" drinking appears to be a common phenomenon in societies where egalitarian features are predominant. As will be demonstrated later, equality and an ethos of sharing as cultural imperatives are strong factors in the drinking styles of many individuals whose traditions are from hunting and gathering societies.

The commonly held view that drinking for Indians is normative, anxiety reducing, identity seeking, or a "time-out" period from a dismal and frustrating social environment is seen in certain evaluations (Dozier 1966; Lemert 1954, 1958; Lurie 1971; MacAndrew and Edgerton 1969). Perhaps this may be true for other ethnic groups. Many of these analyses have pointed to diverse cultural factors. Still, despite these interpretations, the commonly held stereotype that Indians "can't hold their liquor," or have peculiar biological propensity for booze, predominates in Indian-white relationships.

In an extremely perceptive book on Indian-white relationships in the northern Plains, Braroe (1975) attests to the continuing perception of Indians as drunks when he quotes a white Canadian as saying, "There's nothing special about them, they're just a bunch of drunks" (123). He further notes, "Now, drinking is one of the faults whites most frequently single out in censuring Indians, and every Indian is aware of this. Indeed, it is expressed to them by whites in numerous contexts—sometimes contemptuously and sometimes sympathetically, in subtle and not so subtle ways" (139).

Closer to the land of the Lakota, Daniels (1970) reports a common viewpoint of those persons who interact with the Pine Ridge Sioux:

> It is also generally held by whites that the prohibition of alcohol on the reservation (a decision of the tribal council) does not really apply to non-Indians (because, unlike Indians, whites can "hold their liquor"). Alcoholic beverages can be found in the homes of many of the school teachers (where "real Indians" are almost never invited); the Pine Ridge town dump, serving federal personnel, contains an extraordinary number of beer cans (where anyone can observe them). (207)

One can add many such statements found throughout the texts of ethnographies (Basso 1970; Rohner and Rohner 1970). A more recent ethnography carries forth the theme:

> But on payday, people celebrate; young people especially gather in groups and "go on a toot," often lasting the entire night or an entire weekend. Come Monday, some do not make it back to work, resulting in their being fired. Worse yet, their non-Indian employers accuse them of "drinking up their paychecks" and not valuing their jobs. . . . These non-Indians claim

that they are unreliable and are not serious about keeping their jobs. The result is that the already scarce jobs become scarcer. And the racial prejudice, already rampant, develops into bitter hatred. (Grobsmith 1981, 112)

MacAndrew and Edgerton's 1969 book *Drunken Comportment* has done much to destroy such myths and to give new insights into American Indian alcohol consumption patterns. More recent studies (Leland 1976; Levy and Kunitz 1974) have presented new and important cross-cultural viewpoints derived from intensive analyses of certain tribes. Leland takes the Jellinek (1952) points of alcohol addiction and relates ethnographic descriptions from the literature to each point. Levy and Kunitz concentrate principally upon the Navajo with contrastive data from the Hopi and White Mountain Apache in the American Southwest. A startling point indicates that the Hopi tend to imbibe privately, which is in opposition to the heavy public drinking patterns among the Navajo. Rates of cirrhosis of the liver are greater for the Hopi. The White Mountain Apache (like their relatives, the Navajo) evidenced institutionalized public drinking leading to intoxication. This group still brews an aboriginal maize drink, *tiswin* or *tulapai*, for certain ritual events such as the girl's puberty ceremony. They also indicate the highest rates of homicide, suicide, and acts of individual aggression. Moreover, they had higher rates of cirrhosis than the Navajo, but not as high as the Hopi (Levy and Kunitz 1974, 180). Traditional social structure, continuation of the native belief system, and diet are all factors for further exploration.

A careful examination of approximately nine hundred studies on Indian drinking practices indicates that abstinence and the rationale for nonindulgence are almost totally ignored. A caveat seems in order for Westermeyer (1974), who indicates that:

> when considering such specific alcohol-related events, we have considerable evidence that all American Indians do not comprise a single group concerning which generalizations can be made. Considerable differences exist among tribes, even taking into account the small populations of some tribes that make reliable intertribal comparisons difficult. Also within tribes there are subgroup differences. These differences, and the reasons for them, have been neglected in most studies so far. (30)

Most current research indicates that Indian alcoholism is a major social problem. That it has assumed epidemic proportions in many American Indian communities and urban areas is an accepted fact. The *Final Report* of the American Indian Policy Review Commission (1977) indicates: "The most severe and widespread health problem among Indians today is alcoholism and its medical consequences, cirrhosis of the liver. The social problems caused by alcoholism create an environment from which alcohol often seems the only escape" (373). This suggests the problem is of a cyclical nature. A report by the Task Force on Indian Alcoholism of the Indian Health Service (1977) succinctly poses the extent of the situation. It states:

Alcoholism is a costly proposition in every sense of the word. Personal health may be impaired by cirrhosis and its complications, neuropsychiatric disorders and nutritional deficiencies. The majority of accidents, especially fatal ones are associated with alcohol, as are nearly all the homicides, assaults, suicides and suicide attempts among Indians. The loss of personal freedom and productivity, the breakup of families, the hardship and humiliation involved are considerable, although not easily measured. (5)

The magnitude of the Indian drinking problem is further indicated in a tabulation by Stewart (1964) that notes that federal crime statistics indicate the proportion of Indians arrested for alcohol-related crimes is twelve times greater than the national average and higher than any other ethnic category. In a study which spanned the years 1950 to 1968, Reasons (1972) indicates that the arrest rate for Indians was three times that of blacks and ten times that of whites. He found that Indians are overrepresented in federal and state prisons, with many of their crimes alcohol related. The litany of family disorganization, suicides, homicides, accidents, and inter- and intragroup violence is repetitive in almost all the reports of native alcohol consumption. These dismal facts make efforts at prevention a necessity. While most American Indians operate a lifestyle below the poverty level and reside in economically depressed areas, alcohol utilization patterns still must be specifically defined for each area of the country.

So the myth persists; the drunken Indian image pertains to all Indians—male and female. It is part of the fabric of white and Indian relationships in the past and the present. While patterns of alcohol utilization, behavior while drinking, and attitudes toward liquor vary from group to group, the image of the aborigines who are "unable to hold their liquor" endures (Leland 1976; MacAndrew and Edgerton 1969; Westermeyer 1974). It is possible, however, to put the use of alcohol in a contextual frame. This is the object of the next chapter, for many individuals are unaware of the history of American Indian alcohol use.

Note

I have chosen not to use standard orthographic markers (IPA) demarcating Lakota phonemes. Thus, for *wasicu*, I have followed the more common accepted *washichu*, ch for c, and gh for X (guttural). This may allow for greater comprehension in view of contemporary use of the Lakota language on the Sioux reservations. This also removes the linguistic notations from orthographic controversy and meets the needs of the Lakota people who are monolingual in the English language.

Uncorking the Keg
Beginnings of Alcohol Use
among American Indians

IN VIEW OF THE MANY ASSUMPTIONS and subjective statements about "drunken Indians," alcohol use in the aboriginal world needs clarification. A backdrop of alcohol absence or presence in the ethnographic record for different tribes will facilitate an understanding of this controversial issue. The production of alcoholic beverages is tied to obvious variables, such as the availability of resources to allow for its production. The Lakota Sioux, as a hunting and gathering society, did not have access to materials to manufacture alcohol. However, another hunting society, the Apache, did manufacture alcohol.

In the American Southwest, the imbibing of alcoholic beverages assumed aspects of rituals. Among the Apache, women made *tiswin* before the reservation period (Flannery 1932). Curley (1967) indicates that men assumed its preparation after 1873. Levy and Kunitz (1974) note:

> The Western Apaches are thought to have made a cactus beer before their initial contacts with the Spanish, although maize beer diffused northward probably about a century ago. In any event, the manufacture of a fermented beer and its secular use was noted as an important problem among the Western Apaches immediately after the establishment of the reservation by early administrators. (62)

Basso (1970) indicates that among the Cibecue Apache, women make the intoxicant *talpi* (tulapai) that is now used in a ceremonial context in the girl's puberty rite (*Nai'es*). This is one example of imbibing native-brewed alcohol within a ritual framework. The above information on a hunting and gathering Athapaskan-speaking society, with clan organization and a previous warrior complex, indicates that in the history of alcohol use within such a group, the sociological features and sex roles pertaining to the manufacture of alcohol, confinement on the reserve, and the patterns of aboriginal consumption are necessary factors to understand the current conditions. Studies by R. M. Boyer (1964), L. B. Boyer (1964), and Curley (1967) stress deviancy and imply a deficit scene: lack of responsibility in adults, absence of effective role models, ineffective socialization practices, dependency upon government, and other "culture of poverty" syndromes. L. B. Boyer's descriptions of drunken behavior are extreme but may characterize drunken aggression in many areas where American Indians presently reside.

However, it is only when the use of intoxicating beverages and the resultant behavior is placed within a total and dynamic cultural context that one will be able to assess its integral part in native cultures. For the Apache, Basso (1966) notes that the use of *tulapai*, the native beer, is a means of cementing reciprocal relations with clan relatives. Basso (1970) speaks of the impact of wage work in the purchase of beer and wine, behavioral responses (silence) to drunken verbal abuse, and the reactions to drunken Apaches at ceremonials. These are instances of native responses to alcohol use in present-day societies. These attempts to utilize native views of drinking behavior offer interesting interpretations. He utilizes native terms to give an insider's viewpoint. Based on my formulation of native categories of Siouan drinking terms, this statement from Everett (1980) amplifies the cognition aspect of Apache drinking:

> For White Mountain Apaches, people either "drink" or they do not. Potentially, it can be said of any individual, "he drinks" or "she doesn't drink." "He used to drink" is also a common and quite meaningful description. For the Anglo observer, confusion is generated when it is discovered that the label for "drink," *iidlaa'*, is normally used with an object to indicate consumption of nonalcoholic beverages, while in isolation it always refers to liquor of some kind. When one Apache says to another, "Do you want a drink?" there is no mistaking the alcohol referent. The semantic domain *iidlaa'* is thus partitioned in the following way. To the query "iidlaa' date-hii?" ("drink, what kinds are there?"), Apaches usually respond by numerating various alcoholic beverages. Thus, even though the category *iidlaa'* consists of both alcoholic and nonalcoholic beverages at the most specific level of discrimination, there appear to be two covert, unlabeled categories corresponding to this dichotomy. (153)

Regularized and ritual use of a fermented drink made from the fruit of the saguaro cactus is a long-standing tradition among the Pima and Tohono O'odham (formerly Papago) Indians of Arizona. Underhill (1953) states, in reference to maize cultivation:

> Perhaps their first ceremony should be called "impregnation" rather than "birth," for it was at this time, just before the summer rains, that the juice of the giant cactus was fermented and drunk with solemn ritual. Such ceremonial drinking, we have mentioned, was widespread in Mexico and South America, but, before white arrival, it was not practiced north of the border except by the Pimans. Their belief was that, as men saturated themselves with liquor, so the earth would be saturated with moisture. In a short time after the drinking festival, the rains came. (196)

Waddell (1971) has indicated that among the contemporary Tohono O'odham, social bonds between males are important considerations in examining drinking styles. Contextually, the drinking pattern presents a fourfold dimension—with family in the home, the wine ceremonial (*nawait*), other festive occasions, and convivial drinking of an idiosyncratic nature. In an urban environment, Waddell (1975) found that "social credit," that is, sharing alcohol, was the basis for an egalitarianism that met the needs of Tohono O'odham migrants and further fostered personal power. The cultural matrix is significant and points to different manifestations of drinking styles.

In contrast to this ritual use, in the prolific literature on American Indian drinking, despite the focus on a certain tribe, or the use or nonuse of alcohol in precontact days, drinking patterns today are most often seen as deviant patterns of alcohol use. Most of the studies deal with an unspecified number of persons, usually male, in urban situations. The only exceptions to this are the long-range studies on the Navajo by Levy and Kunitz (1971a, 1971b, 1974).

Use among Siouan Bands

"Ardent spirits" were absent in culture areas outside the Southwest. This was especially true for the native groups in the northern Plains of North America. For the various bands of the Lakota Sioux, introduction to alcohol coincided with the traders' gradual ascent of the Missouri, roughly between 1790 and 1830 (Saum 1965, 50). It is virtually impossible to designate with precision when liquor was introduced to the Hunkpapa and

Sihasapa bands of the Lakota. Their location removes them from the early trading in the South. Denig (1961) states:

> The *Hoc pa pas, Se ah sap pas,* and *Estas epe chos* occupy nearly the same district. They are so often encamped near each other and conjoined in their operations as scarcely to admit of being treated separately. That part of the country under their control is along the Moreau, Cannon Ball, Heart, and Grand Rivers, seldom extending very far up on Grand River but of late years reaching to the Little Missouri in company with or stationed near the band last described. (25)

The band last described by Denig was the *Min ne con zus*. It can be suggested that these bands were not as involved in the early trading as the southern bands, *Oglala* and *Sicangu*.

That the early exposure to alcohol had devastating effects upon these bands is evident in some of the historical accounts. Many sources of information on the fur trade (Chittenden 1902; Saum 1965; and others) indicate a heightened competition between trading companies after 1834. Hyde (1961) notes:

> It was the coming of John Jacob Astor's American Fur Company into the Sioux country, after the War of 1812, that started bitter competition. The French traders were fighting the Americans; both sides had recourse to the use of bad liquor in their efforts to keep their trade going and to win Sioux camps away from rival companies. The Sioux could not resist the poison that was being offered to them; and from some years before the time of Spotted Tail's birth, the Sioux camps were scenes of drunken riot. Red Cloud's father died during this period, a victim of the traders' bad liquor. The Brulés—demoralized by drink—were also often hungry; for game on the White River now showed plain indications of being hunted out. (25–26)

It cannot be overemphasized that supplying liquor to the Indians was such a lucrative and pervasive part of the fur trade. Saum (1965) relates: "In 1832 when Kenneth McKenzie felt the pinch of the government liquor policy on the upper Missouri he peevishly complained to a colleague that he was neither able or willing 'to bear the onus of debarring my old friends of their dearest comfort.' . . . 'The King of the Missouri' could hardly have been less convincing" (14).

It is not often recognized, however, that a potent means of degradation was set in motion. After noting that Kenneth McKenzie had signed trading agreements with Blackfeet and Assiniboine, Nelson (1946) indicates the following:

> This notable feat accomplished, McKenzie turned to other methods of increasing the company's dominance of the Northwest. In July 1832 Congress had passed stringent laws intended to keep liquor out of the Indian country; inspectors were placed along the upper river at various points to search all boats engaged in the fur traffic; and McKenzie found himself unable to secure his most important article of trade. Some of his competitors were smuggling it overland, and the British companies were enjoying a considerable advantage as a result of the new regulations.
>
> But McKenzie was a resourceful man. Noting that the law merely prohibited the "introduction" of liquor into the Indian country, he constructed a huge still at Fort Union, and with native corn from the Mandan villages began the manufacture of a product that proved quite effective as any imported brand. Envisioning an expansion of his activities, he sent men to the Iowa country to buy land, plant corn and arrange for the transport of the grain upriver to his wilderness distillery. (85–86)

Congress amended the law to prohibit the manufacture of alcohol, but the traders began to intensify their bootlegging activities. Various means of subterfuge were used to transport liquor. Larpenteur (1962), a trader, when referring to the 1833–1834 period in his journal, writes, "It must be remembered that liquor, at that early day, was the principal and most profitable article of trade, although it was strictly prohibited by law, and all the boats on the Missouri were thoroughly searched on passing Fort Levenworth" (57–58). He also verified the operation of a distillery at Fort Union as he vividly describes a trading episode:

> Early in the fall trade commenced, principally in jerked buffalo meat and tallow, both mostly traded for liquor. The liquor business, which was always done at night, sometimes kept me up all night turning out drunken Indians, often by dragging them out by arms and legs. Although the still house had been destroyed, the Company found means to smuggle plenty of liquor. (74)

The natives to whom he referred were the Assiniboine, a Siouan speaking group, and the Cree, an Algonkian tribe, who interacted with the American Fur Company. Later, Larpenteur recounts a trading trip to a group of Cree Indians near Woody Mountain in Canada:

> I sent for water, telling the Indians it was to make fire-water, and it was not long in forthcoming; the news circulated through the camp, and before I

was prepared to trade the lodge was full of Indians, loaded with robes, ready for a spree. The liquor trade commenced with a rush, and it was not long before the whole camp was in a fearful uproar; but they were good Indians and there was no more trouble than is usual on such occasions. (191)

He netted 150 fine robes that night, and during the day, he obtained "30 more for goods." Larpenteur never specified exactly what the goods entailed. Mention is made of a few items, such as a "cotillion," which is footnoted to mean "a piece of dress goods for women's wear, woven in black-and-white" (205). Ammunition and tobacco were standard items, as were trinkets. Coues, the journal editor, defines goods as "flimsy cloth and such trinkets as beads, hawk-bells, red paint, and hand looking-glasses" (195).

Larpenteur (1962) continues with a description of a trading interaction that did occur in the camp of the Crees (after he sent his helper to retrieve a keg of alcohol): "And another glorious drunk took place; but the robe trade was light, only 50 in number. This ended the business, there being no liquor and hardly any robes in camp" (195). The severity of this winter trip is indicated by the fact that the trader's mules froze to death in an upright position. The tragedy of the robeless Crees can only be imagined. In still another revealing vignette, he describes a scene at Fort Williams:

> The liquor trade started at dark, and soon the singing and yelling commenced. The Indians were all locked up in the fort, for fear that some might go to Fort Union, which was but 2½ miles distant. Imagine the noise—upward of 500 Indians, with their squaws, all drunk as they could be, locked up in the small space. The old devil Gauché had provided himself with a pint tin cup, which I know he did not let go during the whole spree, and every now and then he would rush into the store with his cup, and it was "Co-han"—telling me to fill it—and "Co-han! Hurry up about it, too!" This was a great night, but I wished the old rascal and his band had gone to the big fort. At last daylight came and the spree abated; a great many had gone to sleep, and the goods trade did not commence until the afternoon; but old Co-han, with his cup, kept on the move pretty much of the time. It was not until midnight that the trade was entirely over, and early the next morning they moved away, with the exception of the old man and a few of his staff of loafing beggars. (58–59)

Sage (1860) gives an account of the intoxicants themselves:

> The liquor used in this business is generally third or fourth proof whiskey, which, after being diluted by a mixture of three part water, is sold to the

Indians at the exorbitant rate of three cups per robe—the cups usually holding about three gills each. But, notwithstanding the above unconscionable price, a large share of the profits result from the ingenious roguery of those conducting the trade. Sometimes the measuring-cup is not more than half full; then, again the act of measuring is little other than mere feint (the purchaser receiving not one fourth the quantity paid for). When he becomes so intoxicated as to be unable to distinguish the difference between water and liquor (a thing not rare), the former is passed off upon him as the genuine article. Another mode of cheating is, by holding the cup in such a manner that the two front fingers occupy a place upon the inside, and thus save the trader nearly a gill at each filling.

Some have two cups (one the usual size, and the other less), which are so exchanged as to induce the purchaser to believe he is obtaining a third more than he actually receives; and others, yet more cunning, fill the measure half full of tallow and deal out the liquor from off it—the witless dupes, not thinking to examine the bottom, supposes he received the requisite quantity. (121–22)

A gill is a unit of measurement equal to one-fourth pint or one-half cup. It was not possible to ascertain the potency of "third or fourth proof whiskey."

Besides diluting the whiskey—of whatever strength—with water, other substances were added. Laudanum, a tincture of opium, was the most common ingredient used. Larpenteur (1962) indicates that at one time he added laudanum to the drinks of inebriated "half-breeds" to stop a family fight. Chittenden (1902) also mentions its use. The American Fur Company, besides having one of its own employees appointed as an Indian agent on Laramie Fork, also engaged in altering its liquor stock. Hyde (1937), relying upon letters of another Indian agent, Andrew Drips, writes, "The American Fur Company, as it was said at the time, [was] drugging its stock of liquor, probably by adding laudanum to it. This was supposed to be a humane practice, as such drink usually stupefied the Indians and prevented quarrels and killings" (53). In delineating aspects of a trade war between Pratte, Cabanne and Company and the American Fur Company on the Laramie Fork in the Upper Platte region, he gives information about the Sioux:

At first traded at high prices, as competition increased liquor was given to the Indians without charge. The Oglalas had already been through a trade-war of this kind on the Upper Missouri about the year 1822, and had seen scores of their tribesman killed in drunken brawls. These poor Indians knew that liquor was a very bad thing, and most of them did not wish to have it brought to their camps, but when it was pressed upon them they did not have the moral strength to refuse it. Beginning about 1840, this struggle among the traders kept the Oglalas, Brulés, and Cheyennes of the Upper Platte in a state of utter demoralization for several years. In ordinary times the killing of a Sioux by a fellow-tribesman was an event of rare occurrence, but with liquor entering the camps freely such murders happened every day. The lists of killings recorded in the winter counts and by Rufas Sage is appalling, and it is evident that these accounts tell only a portion of the sordid story. (Hyde 1937, 52)

The southern Siouan bands experienced a period of stress after the War of 1812. They were used as pawns by the American Fur Company and its French competitors, as evidenced in published reports (Sage 1860; Chittenden 1902; Hyde 1937; Saum 1965). An established pattern, exploitation of indigenous peoples by mercantile enterprises, is further described with regard to the Brule band of the Lakota:

As was always the case when competition for Indian trade was keen, the rival companies made free use of liquor. They drenched the Sioux camps with alcohol; they sold it at a loss and even gave it away in kegs to the Sioux to win them away from rival traders. Another period of drunken sprees, accompanied by killings and accidental deaths, struck the Sioux camps. It was just what had happened on White River when Spotted Tail was a baby; and now, when he was in his late teens, the same debauchery of his tribe was being repeated. It is said that he and many of the young Brulés took a pledge that they would never taste liquor, and they kept their word. The efforts of government agents to stop the flow of liquor to the Sioux camps was of little avail; but changes in the Indian trade put a stop to this illicit traffic, and by 1844 conditions were better. Indians could still obtain drink, but they had difficulty in getting it. They had to deal with traders of bad repute, and they had to pay a very high price for the stuff. (Hyde 1961, 33)

Resistance to Alcohol Consumption

Pertinent to an understanding of alcohol use is the resistance by some of the Lakota groups to alcohol and its entry into the camps. Of course, the historic accounts very often give the impression that all native people succumbed willingly to drinking intoxicants. Of greater import is that at this time, Lakota persons—males—were opposed to drinking and vowed to avoid it. The pledge in traditional Lakota society was a powerful binding force. Abstinence by choice is of great significance. "Pledging" was a strong motivational force in the self-direction and personal autonomy of males. Though not specifically defined in the ethnographic literature (Provinse 1937; MacGregor 1945), vows had strong supernatural connotations. A vow to perform any deed was an indication of individual decision making and self-actualization. The very essence of masculinity (*bloka*) was engendered in a pledge to go on a war expedition or dance in the sacred Sun Dance with a vow to be pierced or to offer bits of skin from the arms for the good of self and society. Fulfillment of a vow was an imperative. Male participants petitioned for such things as success in war and the hunt, for the health of family members, or for the general well-being of the *tiospaye* (extended family) or band.

The determination to maintain sobriety was made plain by Spotted Tail, who refused to bring his band to obtain rations at Whetstone Agency on the Missouri River. Apparently, the camps near the agency were supplied with whiskey smuggled across the river into the Indian lands. Even in those days, a situation of legal jurisdiction allowed for transgressions. Many of the early maps of the area indicate so-called whiskey ranches on the east bank of the Missouri River that supplied intoxicants to Indians at the agencies. Hyde (1961) notes that "there was no money in the Indian camps. The whiskey trade was barter, mainly for government rations, clothing, and other supplies, and a Sioux who had acquired a taste for drink would strip his family naked and leave it to starve to satisfy his craving" (145). Besides rations, richly quilled or beaded clothing or other decorated items formed part of the barter.

Again, an illicit exchange pattern is evidenced. Based upon barter, some white men (oftentimes married to Indian women, and called "squawmen") established dwellings beyond the Indian agent's control. Trading for U.S. issue such as clothing, blankets, flour, and bacon, in exchange for liquor, often was their livelihood. Hyde (1961) informs us that this illegal trade also happened at Red Cloud Agency in 1871–1872, across the frozen Platte River.

Hyde locates another whiskey ranch fifteen miles below Whetstone Agency and fifteen miles above the Yankton Sioux Agency. Poole (1881) describes an episode in which a Brule, named Big Mouth, had been trading for liquor with a white rancher who was married to a Lakota woman. The Brule man could not continue trading with the rancher, for he had no trade materials or credit. With a party of warriors, he chased the rancher and his wife out, consumed a barrel of whiskey, and demolished the cabin. Hyde (1961) notes that Spotted Tail, the Brule chief, was invited at one time to a feast at Big Mouth's lodge. Big Mouth pressed liquor upon the chief, who refused to drink. As Spotted Tail left, he was pursued by Big Mouth, who tried to shoot him. In the ensuing struggle, Big Mouth was killed. Two companions accompanying Spotted Tail immediately counted coup on the dead man. It is apparent that abstinence was not an easy road in the early days on the reservation. Beside idiosyncratic events such as these, there is insufficient data to show intracultural variations in either drinking patterns or abstention for this period.

However, the pressure to promote the utilization of alcohol was ongoing. Evidence of the pursuit of Indians for the whiskey trade is graphically portrayed by O'Reilly (1889):

> The Indians had for some times past been stealing horses from the whites, and now had a number of very fine animals. We could get a horse worth two hundred and fifty dollars for a gallon of tarantula juice, and the project was to go out and trade with them in this commodity. Any qualms of conscience I may at one time have had, as to the iniquity of trading whiskey with redskins, had long since vanished. The mischief had already been done by others, and if they could not get it from one source they would from another. As this was the principal commodity upon which trading negotiations were conducted, I thought I might just as well be in the swim as not. It was a difficult time to keep the Indians in the Reservation; they were running all over the place and there were more out than in. We got a few wagons together, laid in a good stock of fire-water, and moved out into the open on the look-out for wandering parties. We ran across several of these, and did fairly well for some time. The Indians would sell anything for whiskey, and parted readily with horses and mules, which had cost them nothing, for a few drinks. (320–21)

The Indians referred to in the above passage, which undoubtedly is slightly exaggerated, were Lakota of the Oglala and Brule bands.

The promotion of alcohol consumption proceeded unabated from the Fur Trade era, through the early reservation period, and into the present by a variety of novel means and with a blatant disregard for legal controls to protect the native people from a pernicious product. The above descriptions give an awareness of the pressures exerted upon the Lakota bands in the south. No information exists for the northern bands.

Alcohol was a powerful tool in the process of "civilizing" American Indians through the mercantile enterprise of European powers vying for profit (Bishop 1974; Debo 1970; Hickerson 1956; Ray 1978; Saum 1965). Tribes of all areas were eventually affected in a manner that was not beneficial to their well-being.

Alcohol was not a gift of the devil, as stated among the native-evolved proscriptions in the Iroquois Code of Handsome Lake (Wallace 1969), but was a tool of oppressors. Used as a potent item of trade, alcohol was effective in gaining furs, food, women, and land for European interests.

This brief overview of the use of alcohol in aboriginal North America includes its function and dimensions. It also draws attention to the introduction of intoxicating substances to native groups who had no previous experience with such consciousness-altering items. Factors of trade and frontier economics established a series of symbiotic relationships that persist to the present time.

The Recent Past

3

Minnewakan "Magic Water"—
Alcohol and the Lakota Bands

A	S THE PREVIOUS BRIEF ethnohistorical account indicates, the introduction of a foreign psychoactive agent—alcohol—with a purely mercenary motivation on the part of the introducers, originated initial and subsequent abuse among indigenous populations. The advent of alcohol without accompanying standards of behavior (much less a ritualized form and codified manner of ingestion, as with peyote) fostered distinct drinking styles. A much quoted study of an intertribal nature by MacAndrew and Edgerton (1969) suggests that native drunken comportment, characterized by "mayhem and debauchery" (137), was patterned after the behavior of early traders and frontiersmen who introduced liquor. The drunken and explosive conduct exhibited by natives indicated a process of socialization to drinking demeanor that seems to have persisted. Patterns of disruption and discord, and the resultant disastrous repercussions, appear to have been established. This chapter will outline the major social, political, and economic consequences that have been amplified in many of the Lakota Sioux reservations in North and South Dakota.

The existence of various studies dealing with the Lakota Sioux necessitates that the native population be defined. The Western Sioux, also referred to as the Teton Lakota, were traditionally comprised of the Seven Council Fires (*Ocheti Shakowin*), which could be designated as a tribe. Tribe is the social organizational gloss that is recognized by the Lakota people themselves. The term gives substance to loosely formed and flexible smaller social structural units called bands. The named bands were, and are, important identity markers and mediate between the larger unit and the *tiospaye* (extended family). The named bands were, and are, the *Oglala* ("Scatter

One's Own"); *Sichangu* ("Burnt Thighs"); *Minneconjou* ("Plant by the Water"); *Oehenonpa* ("Two Boilings" of "Two Kettle"); *Itazipcho* ("Without Bows"); *Sihasapa* ("Blackfoot"); and the *Hunkpapa* ("Those Who Camp at the Entrance"). French terms for the Sichangu and the Itazipcho were Brulé and Sans Arcs respectively, and the terms are interchangeable in the ethnographic literature (MacGregor 1945; Provinse 1937).

These bands or tribal subdivisions currently are meaningful to the people living on the Sioux reservations. Individuals and *tiospaye* identities are bound to these named social units in the native language. At present, the terms Sioux and Lakota are used interchangeably, as has been done in historic records and anthropological reports. In addition, one hears band designations and reservation names used as ethnic markers and methods of placing individuals. Thus, "Standing Rock Sioux" or Hunkpapa Lakota may be examples of denotations of individuals.

Generally, the present-day reservation system follows the assignments of bands to these parcels of lands, mainly in South Dakota. Certain bands were assigned to each reservation. Thus, Pine Ridge Reservation is mainly occupied by the descendants of the Oglala bands. Sichangu (Brule) people reside on the Rosebud Reservation. Cheyenne River Reservation is populated by the descendants of the Minneconjou, Oehenonpa, and the Itazipcho. Members of the Hunkpapa and Sihasapa bands are presently living on the Standing Rock Reservation, which extends into North Dakota where the agency center, Fort Yates, is located. However, there are some members of eastern bands, mainly *Yanktonais*, who also were assigned to Standing Rock. They speak the Dakota dialect of their eastern forebears and maintain a dialectical island among the other Lakota-speakers (Medicine 1979).

The introduction of intoxicants to these different bands varied greatly. The ethnohistorical literature indicates that liquor had a sustained consumption pattern among the southern bands, such as Brule and Oglala. A comparison of the range and intensity of consumption throughout all of the Siouan bands is difficult to assess, and historical materials for the Minneconjou or the Sihasapa are scarce.

It can be surmised that the liquor trade intensified after 1834 for the majority of the Sioux bands. New trading companies entered the field and intense rivalry exerted greater pressure to keep the Lakota under control by dispensing liquor. Despite long-standing constraints upon the sale of liquor to Indians, there was a strong tradition of surreptitious trade. Historical accounts often give the impression that all Indians were drunken puppets. There is evidence, and it is corroborated by MacAndrew and Edgerton

(1969, 117), that all tribes of the northern Plains were not "naturally" prone to drinking. The Arikara, a riverine tribe located on the Missouri River, did not initially imbibe. Further, Denig (1930) comments about the tribes of the Upper Missouri, where he resided for twenty-one years, that "they all drink when they can get it—men, women, and children—except the Crow Indians will not taste it" (529). Patterns of availability are difficult to determine for the early contact period.

As fragmented and dispersed as the data for the early reservation period appear, for most of the Lakota Sioux groups the era from 1900 onward is even more lacking in material regarding drinking patterns. Commissioner of Indian Affairs reports for the period are filled with estimates of how many Lakota were "wearing civilized or citizen's dress," how many were Christianized, or how many marriages were no longer polygamous. Oral history reports indicate that for many Lakota males their first experience with alcohol was during their volunteered service in World War I. Though this chosen entry into the service of their country endowed them with citizenship before it was granted to the rest of the Indian population in 1924, the service did not confer access to the purchase and use of alcohol on them as returned veterans. This war experience, however, gave them prestige in the latent honoring system that still respected warriors. Nevertheless, it put them in an anomalous position as landowners and taxpayers. In the impoverished positions of the reservations, many were unable to pay taxes on trust land, which then went out of Indian ownership. The veterans of World War I comprised a sizeable group. On Standing Rock, estimates of the number of communities with populations of one hundred to one hundred fifty male household heads range from ten to fifteen veterans. The experience away from the reservations allowed them to cater to a newly acquired taste. When this thirst quenching was satisfied in border towns, there was often a polite "looking the other way" by some of the white officers of the law. They, after all, had defended their country, and many of the Indian males were classified as "good" Indians and taxpayers. It seems, also, that it was during this period that some veterans and their wives experimented with making wines from wild chokecherries, June berries, and wild plums. Some made a type of home-brewed beer. This enterprise did not assume great proportions in Indian communities as it did in other parts of North America (Hara 1980; Honigmann and Honigmann 1945). It was during the 1920s and 1930s that a small minority of Lakota people drank such items as vanilla and lemon extracts, perfume, and shaving lotion. These were utilized sporadically when true alcoholic spirits were unavailable, and often after a "drunk."

Congress had adopted legislation in the Act of March 30, 1802, that authorized the president "to take such measures, from time to time, as to him may appear expedient to prevent or restrain the vending or distributing of spirituous liquors among all or any of the said Indian tribes, anything herein contained to the contrary notwithstanding" (Cohen 1942, 352). Stringent restrictions were also to be enforced by the Indian Trade and Intercourse Act of 1834. This policy was directed toward the exploitative practices of the fur trade and was often circumvented by unscrupulous traders and Indian agents. This protective legislation remained in effect until 1953, when Public Law 277 signed by President Eisenhower changed "discriminatory liquor laws as they pertain to Indians" (Tyler 1973, 316). This allowed tribal members to purchase and consume intoxicants of any alcoholic content and to drink in public places, such as bars and taverns. Some tribes, however, voted for options allowing continued prohibitions on their reservations. Some of the reservations are still "dry" today as a result. This fact alone makes for tremendous differences in drinking styles and consumption patterns across tribes in the present day.

The increased and concentrated use of alcohol began in earnest among most Lakota people on all reservations after the 1953 prohibitory edict was lifted. This was also the beginning of the concentration of studies on alcohol use in all tribes. This era might be seen as a period of aberrant utilization. Though President Eisenhower might be looked upon as a folk hero in some parts of the native world for his stand on issues of equity, most Indians agree that the excessive use of alcohol stemming from that period had been debilitating to individuals and communities.

The fact that legal restrictions were placed upon all Indians in the United States from 1802 to 1953 speaks to a legal validation of the myth that "Indians can't hold their liquor." It also reified the notion that wild, uncontrolled behavior as a consequence of drinking alcoholic beverages was normative. In a sense, the fact that drinking alcohol had to be legally controlled points to the second-class citizenship that has been the lot of Indians in North America.

The use of liquor to gain advantage in trade with the southern bands of the Sioux was extensive. Exploitation of native peoples in the northern Plains resulted in adaptations to various degrees in a change process throughout this culture area. Factors other than liquor were, of course, also significant. Such external impositions as new belief systems, changes in family structure, linguistic and religious repression, and new economic patterns are all factors for consideration. All these variables may have contributed to acculturative stress for native people while adapting to a changing lifestyle.

Winter Counts and Description of Abuse

From the very sparse data describing the early interactions with traders, it can be surmised that the pressure to push alcohol as a trade item was not as intense for the Sihasapa and Hunkpapa bands as it was with the Assiniboines to the northwest or the southern Lakota. It is possible, however, to consult the extant "winter counts" as some seldom utilized sources. One can see that the intake of alcoholic spirits was most direct and immediate. Howard's (1979) compilation of such mnemonic devices records instances from an "emic" perspective. This is instructive for the groups on Standing Rock. He notes, "The pictograph on the British Museum count show a man holding an old-fashioned whiskey bottle, which he has evidently drained" (42). The Lakota statement indicates, "Huksaha, mniwaken'n iyeya na yatka'n ya'n t'a," which translates, "Broken-leg whiskey he-found and drinking he-died." This is for the year 1832–1833. The 1875–1876 period is described by a drawing of a keg. "Mniwaka'n iyeyapi" is translated as "Whiskey they-found." Howard (1979) writes, "The pictograph is a representation of a whiskey keg." The counts of the Blue Thunder group and No Two Horns supply details: Blue Thunder, "Found keg of whiskey at Fort Yates, near the shore. Made a council and drank it all up. Many drunk." Blue Thunder variants I, II, and III indicate, "They found a barrel of whiskey near store at Yates. Had a council and drank it all up. Knew whiskey well. Lots of it before, I drink and was drunk." No Two Horns, "Found a barrel of whiskey. Had a good time." Blue Thunder and No Two Horns show a keg of whiskey set on end with liquor flowing from the bunghole into a cup. Blue Thunder variants I, II, and III merely show a keg, a jug, and a cup in association (396). Vestal's (1934) White Bull count mentions whiskey for the year 1875 but does not include it in the later counts (269). White Bull states that it was given to the treaty party who signed the Black Hills Treaty and that "they were made drunk in order to get them to sign" (Howard 1979, 76).

The incident portrayed in the drawing must have been significant to be included as a year's outstanding event. It indicates that kegs of whiskey were being smuggled into the reservation and suggests that whiskey ranches may also have been operating on the east shore of the Missouri River across from the agency, as they were at Whetstone and Yankton agencies further south. These illustrations might also suggest that the pattern of imbibing intoxicants was quick and that complete utilization occurred. Whether the death could be attributed to the effects of alcohol or the ingredients other than alcohol that might have been added is, of course, uncertain.

The translated term "drank it all up" possibly points to a drinking style in which the liquid is consumed in one sitting. This consumption style may have been common then. These descriptions essentially reaffirm Lakota drinking patterns, which have been suggested for other tribes as well. This pattern of consumption could be reflective of the legal restrictions at that time because imbibing until all the evidence is gone seems a logical act to those drinking illegally.

Traders, Squaw Men, and Abuse: Standing Rock

The major trading post located on Standing Rock used alcohol as a trade item. Oglesby (1963) writes that Joseph Perkins "was put in charge of the company's goods at Franklin. In January, he headed a small expedition to Fort Lisa with some $3,000 worth of merchandise, including 797¾ gallons of that necessary staple, whiskey" (176). In one of the few descriptions of the trading encounter with northern bands, Oglesby (1963) continues:

> Especially, the trader had to have a firm control over his liquor supply, to ration it out in quantities to keep the Indians, who always demanded it, placated, but never in quantities large enough to allow them to get drunk, for there was no greater problem for the trader to cope with than inebriated Indians in and around his post. They were unpredictable, violent, and malicious, inclined to destroy rather than increase trade. (121)

Denig's writings inform us that the Hunkpapa had murdered a trader of the American Fur Company, a Mr. La Chapelle, on the Grand River. The Hunkpapa, Sihasapa, and Itazipcho were generally belligerent to traders. In 1853, they evicted, by flogging, traders who were attempting to build wintering camps. Denig (1961) states, "at the present day the traders cannot safely winter their camps" (27).

Sunder (1963) states that John A. N. Ebbets of New York, representing the Union Fur Company, "concentrated his trade near Fort Pierre during 1840–1841, and sold liquor to Indians" (129). The liquor trade brought trouble from the federal government, but the exact control measures are unknown in this case. Although this fort was below Cheyenne River and Standing Rock agencies, there is little recorded about the whiskey trade at these agencies. However, illegal liquor traffic was a constant difficulty at Standing Rock Agency. There was an apparently subtle conspiracy against its effective enforcement in many forts and agencies. For example, a notorious bootlegger named Reilly was picked up and taken to Fort Abraham Lincoln, near Bismarck, by military escort. The agent had proper witnesses, and he seemed sure to win the case. However, Reilly escaped like so many military prisoners under escort (Milligan 1976). This suggests possible collusion between the military and the bootleggers. A description of a further incident mentions the agency physician's "uproariously drunken and abusive" behavior in Bismarck (Milligan 1976, 82). When reports reached Agent Hughes, he investigated and found the infirmary at the agency in great disorder, with the whiskey and brandy stores quite depleted. It must be recalled that, after the Civil War, being stationed at isolated Indian agencies was not a plum assignment. This is an era of sparse reporting about composition of troops and other ancillary personnel at Indian agencies. In most cases, the biased reports of Indians agents fill the historic records of this era.

Milligan (1976) indicates that some social diversion did exist:

> "Operation Winona" was the most popular river crossing ever made by any unit of the United State Army. The six companies stationed at Fort Yates found the monotony of frontier life relieved by the fifty to a hundred dance hall girls imported from Chicago and other points east, who entertained in the saloons and brothels across the river at Winona, where Ott Black and his wife "Mustache Maude," presided in the most notorious hell hole of them all. By boat in summer, across the ice in winter, these valiant defenders of our nation with valor above and beyond the call of duty made their "nightly assaults" on this citadel of vice in all its lowest forms. (82)

This arrangement did not eliminate the interaction of the troopers and Sioux people at the fort. Owing to the nearness of the barracks to the Indian encampment, Milligan notes several instances of harassment of Sioux women by the soldiers.

So-called squawmen were also troublesome to both Indians and agents. "They stole the wood, which they then sold to the Indians" (Milligan 1976, 89). Additionally, some white men forged passes for Indians to leave the reservation. Others claimed the same rights and privileges as the Lakota people under the Treaty of 1868.

Unfortunately, all the early records of Standing Rock reservation were burned in 1930 when a new agency was built. The records that Milligan used were salvaged by his "adopted sister." Milligan (1976) makes an interesting statement regarding liquor use among the Standing Rock Sioux:

> I have always said that the Indian gave the white man tobacco and made of them chain smokers, but the white man plied the Indian with liquor and made many of them chain drinkers. Liquor was forbidden on the reservation, but on the outer edges the illegal sale of alcoholic beverages

abounded. Trouble developed on the east side of the river because of frequent brawls in which both whites and Indians were victims of gunshot wounds. Bootlegging was a thriving business in the area of military posts and Agencies. Even today where liquor is legal, it thrives on reservations, with whites doing a lucrative business, aided and abetted by Indians and mixed bloods. (22)

In early 1875, squatters on the east side of the Missouri River, opposite Standing Rock Agency, opened a store to sell liquor and other commodities. In early 1875, the president issued an executive order that would break up the liquor traffic on the east side of the river by including the land in the reservation. The Indian agent, Palmer, recommended as a precautionary measure that the northern boundary of the reservation be extended to include the southern bank of the Cannonball River opposite Beaver Creek, where the liquor activities were concentrated. The hub of the liquor trade was north of Beaver Creek and strategically placed for consumption by troopers at Fort Lincoln, Bismarck, and at Fort Rice, below this outpost. It must be stressed that the garrisons of military personnel stationed on reservations were the object of much of the liquor trade. Thus, Milligan (1976) states, "Liquor smugglers now began to use small boats to cross the Missouri and sell their wares west of the river in Indian country. The agent asked the military to cooperate in stopping these illegal acts. He urged the boats crossing the river to be searched for liquor before being allowed to land. But, again, no cooperation was given" (38).

These presentations are not to indicate that the Sioux natives themselves were blameless in the traffic in alcohol. Milligan, in drawing information from primary sources, states: "Brave Bear, who had acquired a strong taste for liquor, made a practice of procuring Indian women as prostitutes for whites connected with the Agency, thereby securing money with which to purchase alcoholic beverages, and Hughes attempted to do away with both Brave Bear's drunkenness and his illegitimate business" (88). As cited in Milligan, the Report of the Commissioner of Indian Affairs (1877) states that "prostitution was confined to a very few women, who consorted with low-grade whites and some of the soldiers whose self-respect and morals were of the lowest order" (73). These statements corroborate oral history reports that prostitution was sometimes resorted to by Lakota women as a means of obtaining food. Referring to early reservation days, Dakota anthropologist Ella C. Deloria states, "Times were hard in those days. Some of the headmen even sold their daughters to the soldiers. Of course, our families didn't" (Medicine 1980, 151).

Scouts (Indian policemen) in the service of the government also were involved in bootlegging liquor. Some names given are Black Eye, Bear Comes Out, Red Hail, Billy Cross, Good Wood, and Shoot Him (Milligan 1976, 51). Trading of all commodities—most specifically guns, ammunition, beads, and alcohol—was a pattern of profiteering for the inhabitants of most forts, and Fort Yates was no exception.

Scattered references to liquor use appear in some ethnographies of the Sioux in more recent times. MacGregor (1945) writes:

> Just over the Nebraska line from Pine Ridge town is White Clay, a drab little village composed largely of stores along either side of the highway. This is the "Gay White Way" for the reservation employees, since they can buy beer there. Although sale of liquor to Indians is forbidden by federal law, the Indians get it through bootleggers. White Clay's beer parlors are its chief attraction, but its stores and garages offer competition to the few in Pine Ridge and draw the business of government and Indians alike. (83)

Owing to the tribal decision not to sell liquor on the Pine Ridge reservation, White Clay still serves as a major distribution point for intoxicants. Moreover, bootleggers thrive on this reservation as they do elsewhere. White Clay is typical of all the other so-called border towns that serve as trading centers for the major Sioux reservations in the Dakotas. It indicates the symbiotic nature of Indian-white relations in the Great Plains.

Schusky describes the illicit liquor trade on Lower Brule reservation during the early 1920s. Duncan, the agent, attempted to control the extensive liquor trade. Schusky (1975) writes:

> When he could get federal officers to arrest a white offender, he believed there was a chance of conviction in federal courts, but he judged that a state arrest and conviction of a white man for victimizing Indians were virtually hopeless. White juries and probably the court officers of the state were not ready to consider Indians the equal of other citizens. (182)

This tension between federal and state law enforcement exists to the present day.

Summary of Social Climate

These instances portray the social climate in such states as North and South Dakota where native peoples interacted with members of the dominant society. Indeed, in these interchanges the onus was usually upon the Indian consumer of liquor. The Indian person was arrested for possession of liquor containers with "an open seal." He was in a quandary, for he was honor bound (in Lakota terms) not to "squeal" and thus to point to the bootlegger. To do so would not only place him in the category of turn-coat but would also ultimately cut off the supply of intoxicants to other tribal members who might be inclined to consume alcohol. The threat of being arrested for having a bottle with a broken seal necessitated the immediate consumption of the liquor contents in order to eliminate the evidence. This immediate and instant consumption of the liquor contents has not been adequately assessed in the contemporary "drinking until devoured" syndrome that is so often pointed to as a drinking pattern of Sioux individuals. In the days before 1953, the surreptitious Indian drinker was in a double bind. Given circumstances of legal restriction, it was impossible for Indian people on the reservations to develop drinking styles approximating patterns of the white middle class. Indeed, in the segregation that existed between whites and Indians, Indians had little awareness of drinking behavior of white persons in border towns. The most intense interaction was with a lower-class white population. White (1970) documents this interaction in the urban center of Rapid City.

Present jurisdictional regulations are important factors in liquor consumption and control. In South Dakota, where the majority of Lakota people reside, some tribal groups, such as the Oglala on Pine Ridge Reservation, prohibit the sale and possession of alcoholic beverages. This fosters the continuance of the bootlegging situation. Other tribes, like Standing Rock Sioux, maintain legal jurisdiction on the reservation or certain parts thereof, while allowing the sale of alcoholic beverages. This legality complicates the enforcement of state laws. State law-enforcing officers have access to some areas of the reservation, while tribal codes and Bureau of Indian Affairs rules are applicable in other areas. This leads to great confusion and lax law enforcement.

In any analysis of contemporary Indian life in modern American society, one is struck by the subordinate status of Indian groups. The dominance of the larger society in the decision-making process is one of the most pervasive aspects of reservation life. Myriad federal, state, and tribal institutions impinge upon the lives of the indigenous populations. From the destruction of the warrior role during reservation beginnings, the forceful push for the males to become farmers (which, in Lakota society, was seen as women's work), to the preferential hiring of Indian women against Indian men in today's workforce, the depreciation of the original provider role has continued. The Lakota males occupy a marginal position in which the constant struggle for self-fulfillment is often obliterated by a drunken haze. Other current analyses of the position of minority men in American society parallel this (Hannerz 1969; Stack 1974).

In the northern plains reservations and the interface with border towns, racial discrimination is prevalent. This means that persons of Indian ancestry cannot easily obtain jobs in these communities. The only available occupations are those connected with governmental agencies, such as the Bureau of Indian Affairs and the U.S. Public Health Service, as well as those with tribal programs, which are based upon federal funding. Nepotism is a strong factor on most reservations—kin-affiliated appointments being extremely prevalent. This is the continuation of the tradition of caring for one's kin in Lakota culture. However, the total effect of these funded programs on the population's economic well-being is negligible.

In the political realm, liquor is used as a vote-getting device in tribal elections (which are part of the relatively new idea of government by Tribal Councils that was initiated by the Indian Reorganization Act of 1934). The implicit rule is a "pint of wine" for one vote. It is not uncommon to observe kin of the candidates hauling (i.e., transporting) the habitué of the neighboring towns (recognized "alcoholics") into the polling places on the reservations. Thus, for a brief time, the habitual drunkards, as they are called by the local Lakota, exhibit their concern for the people—for a price.

That a more rigidly stratified society is emerging on the Lakota reservations seems evident in the political components of contemporary reservation life. There have always been the full-blood (in Lakota, *o-zu*, meaning "full" or "saturated," and *Lakota k'techa*, "ultimate Lakota" or "pure Lakota") and the so-called half-breed (*eyeska*, "translator," or *o ki se*—"half") components on Sioux reservations, resulting in the forming of factions (Daniels 1970; Medicine 1979). This social dichotomy appears to be increasing at the expense of the full bloods, who are on the lowest rungs of the status system in the political sphere but who have an enhanced status in the religious realm. Many are landowners. There are few *O zu ye* (full bloods) who are active in local-level politics, but they tend to serve as tokens in a power game where it benefits them to serve in subservient positions on the Tribal Council. My analysis further illuminates "reservation culture" as described by Useem and Eicher (1970). "Reservation culture" encompasses a range of individuals composed of various degrees of blood quantum, but it also deals with status considerations based on sociopolitical considerations, education, traditionality, and concern for people. Essentially, these variables are operative in a reservation-based "pecking order."

The most blatantly discriminatory aspects of Indian life are connected with the judicial system. On many reservations, the tribal code or the Bureau of Indian Affairs' legal apparatus prevail. On Standing Rock Reservation, and on others in the state of South Dakota, the "checkerboard" system of land use and occupancy exists. White ranchers and farmers and Indian landowners coexist. Therefore, it is often uncertain as to who has legal jurisdiction in some areas of the reservation. This is especially true on Standing Rock, where two state governments operate legal codes. County law enforcement officers have rights in some villages and municipalities and yet cannot interfere on some land areas that are under trust status (in federal control). Clearly, this is a problem, as indicated by a recent hearing of the U.S. Commission on Civil Rights (1977):

> When I sat on courts that had to decide which law governs and which law enforcement agency had jurisdiction, you'd find a reservation that included, say, North and South Dakota, and a different rule in one part of the reservation and another part and it had to be resolved at a higher level. I don't wonder that the American Indian may lack some confidence in the system, but he's part of the problem in the sense the insistence upon the tribal status preserves some of these problems. (Testimony of William Webster, director, Federal Bureau of Investigation, 19)

Similar documents also corroborate instances of police harassment, intimidation, and unlawful arrests (U.S. Commission on Civil Rights 1974, 41–44).

Jurisdictional issues sometimes reach the point of ridiculousness. One case involved a drunken Lakota male who was escaping the municipal police. At issue was the location, at the time of his apprehension, of the main current of the Missouri River, which separates a white municipality from Standing Rock Reservation.

Such an instance highlights the capricious nature of arrests of Sioux drinkers. Murray Wax (1971) makes these comments concerning alcohol use:

> For example, in some small towns neighboring the Pine Ridge Reservation, a high proportion of white drunks are sent home, but Indian drunks are incarcerated and sentenced to labor on public projects. The police might defend themselves on the grounds that, since Indians come from the Reservation, which is dry, to drink in town, they have no "homes" to which they may be sent when drunk. It would, in addition, be a costly service to house them in jail. In areas where police forces utilize "arrest quotas" as devices to keep their men actively patrolling, there is a natural

tendency for some patrolmen to meet their daily quota by victimizing a population that is politically powerless and socially conspicuous in a fashion judged negatively by community leaders. (154)

In analyzing the "Court News" (also facetiously called the "Indian Society Page" by some reservation residents), one finds that items as "Drunk and Disorderly," "Driving While Intoxicated," "Resisting Arrest," "Broken Seal"—all alcohol-related situations—fill the newspaper column. These situations lead to arrests, fines, or confinement in jail. Every Sunday morning, one can observe white ranchers and farmers paying fines for Lakota males. Working in return for payment of fines, Sioux men provide a cheap labor pool for these persons. Whatever the legal entanglements, most of the arrests and convictions of Sioux males are alcohol related.

Powerlessness

That drinking of alcohol by Sioux males is a means of dealing with feelings of powerlessness cannot be denied in view of the social conditions on and off the reservations. Second-class citizenship and the lack of economic and social capital are endemic. That powerlessness is an accurate perception might be noted in the fact that Lakota males often refer to liquor of any kind as "false courage." Drinking alcoholic beverages may be a comfortable way to deal with the social inequities of life on the reservations and in urban areas. It may be an adaptive orientation to a hostile environment, and Lakota males may be loath to abandon it.

Possibly these feelings of inadequacy and demasculinization covertly motivate the continuing resort to alcohol that is noted so strongly in the studies of Lakota drinking styles for males. Early socialization to drinking in order "to be a man" is then continued throughout the masculine experience. A push to drinking conformity is applied by one's drinking buddies or peers—one should drink like a man, and if one refuses, then one is "too good to drink with us."

Mohatt (1972) sought a rationale for Lakota male drinking in the concept of "power." The *wakan*, or power domain, is familiar to most Lakota males. Traditionally, the search for power was a means for self-actualization and self-direction. The *hanblecheya* ("crying for a vision" or vision quest) was an institutionalized means of achieving an altered state of consciousness in order to receive a vision (which was a mandate for action in one's adult life). By fasting, drinking no water, and concentrating upon the *wakan* (the omnipotent power base), the senses were altered.

A visionary "guardian spirit" appeared and became the guide to the future life of the individual male. This search for power does not seem a plausible explanation for male drinking. Lakota males have not gone on vision quests since the belief systems were suppressed in 1882. (There have been attempts at *hanblecheya* since 1965.) Powerlessness, in a socioeconomic domain, does have relevance, however.

For Sioux men on the reservations, the involvement in sharing, especially of alcoholic beverages, and the continued participation in peer groups can be counterproductive and lead to the undermining of marital bonds and job security. The inability to continue caring for their families is not unique in the lives of Lakota men. Lang (1979) and Westermeyer (1972), dealing with lives of Chippewa Indian men, indicate that apathy and continual drinking are major factors in marriage discord. Factors of discrimination and racism are also important variables in the negation of self.

At the risk of being repetitious, and possibly confirming the stereotype of the "drunken Indian," it is imperative that the ethnohistorical roots of the introduction of alcohol to native peoples be reemphasized. Behavior patterns are long lasting and hard to change. The literature depicts surprisingly similar imbibing patterns for the bands cited in this last chapter—periodic, public, extended, loud, and culminating in unfortunate circumstances such as fights. The question nags: how then is this different from lower-class white or black drinking? Impressionistically, this theme might also indicate that in certain classes of the general population, public excessive drinking with resultant aggressive behavior is also prevalent. In general, Lakota drinking tends to be public. It is seen in border towns, at rodeos, and increasingly, at powwows. The frequency of drinking and the amount imbibed in private may be a function of socioeconomic factors. It is my observation, however (and discussed in chapter 5) that tribal members exhibit a variety of drinking styles and that these behavioral options are understood and enacted by members of these social groupings.

A Siouan Social System
Standing Rock Reservation

4

D EMOGRAPHIC DATA FOR reservations inhabited by American Indians has been characterized by lack of precision. Since 1980 the U.S. Census has included a self-ascribed category, and the Census Bureau started making a concerted effort to enumerate American Indians and Alaska Natives. In addition, various government agencies involved in the administration of Indians—such as the Indian Health Service, Housing and Urban Development, Office of Education's (now Department of Education's) Indian Education Division, and the Bureau of Indian Affairs—give population estimates that tend to be at variance with each other. This is owing to such factors as eligibility, place of residence, and enrollment policies. Individual reservations have their own statistics.

The reported total for the American Indian population as of April 1, 1980, was 1,361,869. This indicates an increase of 569,000 persons, or a 72 percent increase since 1970. The Census Bureau indicates that growth is a "result of natural increase and overall improvement in census procedures, including modified enumeration procedures on American Indian reservations and the use of self–identification to obtain the race of the respondents in all areas of the country" (U.S. Census of Populations 1980, 1–2). Of importance to this study is an indication that the American Indian population as a proportion of the total population was highest in New Mexico with 8 percent, with South Dakota being second with 6.5 percent. Other information available indicates an Indian population of 20,119 for North Dakota, which includes seven reservations. As these total figures are not indicated by reservation, it is necessary to utilize the statistics offered by the Manpower Planner, which was directed by the Tribal

Council for reapportionment of the seven districts on Standing Rock Reservation for voting purposes in 1972. An eighth district, McLaughlin, now called Bear Soldier, is now a voting district.

The following information received from the Bureau of Indian Affairs' superintendent indicates a total reservation population of 6,138 (personal communication, 1981). This total indicates enrolled members and gives no indication of those persons who are not resident on the reservation. It also does not address the issue of urbanization. The 1970 census indicates that 55 percent of Indians resided in off-reservation towns or in urban areas. See table 4.1 for a further delineation according to community.

As a growing valuation of Lakota identity becomes evident, the recent name changes are indicated after these communities. Individuals are also changing surnames to more Indian-sounding names, that is, Rick McLaughlin to Rick Red Eagle.

The total population is further divided into 4,301 males and 3,657 females. In the category, designated "adjacent to the reservation," there is a further division of 1,271 males and 549 females. This designation presents interesting interpretations, for it was impossible to obtain the transient rate as opposed to those who resided permanently *off* the reservation. Of a potential labor force of 2,980, 618 were employed, with 591 earning $7,000 or more a year, and 27 persons earning less than that amount. With an educational level of nine years, the unemployment rate was in 1980 estimated to be 60 percent. The income from grazing permits is a major source for most individuals. Ranching is engaged in by a small proportion of the population, with wage labor based upon federal programs targeted for Indians being the mainstay of most families.

Castile (1974) has labeled reservations as "sustained enclaves." Elsewhere, I have used the term "administered human relationships" to characterize reservations (Medicine 1973). A geographical apartness and isolation from the surrounding American society is typical of reservation situations.

Table 4.1. Reservation Populations According to Community

North Dakota		South Dakota	
Community	*Population*	*Community*	*Population*
Cannonball	847	Bull Head, now Rock Creek	692
Ft. Yates, now Long Soldier	1,967	Kenel	259
Porcupine	217	Little Eagle, now Running Antelope	695
		McLaughlin, now Bear Soldier	758
		Wakpala	707
Total	**3,031**		**3,111**

The binding of the eight Sioux communities on Standing Rock by threads of bureaucracies is the prominent characteristic. It is clear that the enclaved community model illuminates the apathy and anomie syndromes that have been reported elsewhere (Levy and Kunitz 1971b). American Indians have a closer relationship with the federal government based, in part, upon treaty agreements made at the time of initial contacts. The picture offered below is ongoing:

> On Indian reservations . . . federal officials actually build and run schools, operate vocational training programs, provide scholarships to Indian students, supply medical care and hospital service, administer sales of minerals and timber, collect rentals, distribute checks to landowners, and supply general welfare assistance to Indian clients. (Officer 1971, 55)

The Standing Rock Reservation is located in Sioux County, North Dakota, and Corson County, South Dakota, encompassing approximately 848,000 acres. However, as the population figures vary, the land base changes—with land going in and out of "trust relationship." That is, land may go out of Indian ownership by sale, or land that has been out of trust and taxed may be turned back to Bureau of Indian Affairs (BIA) supervision and tribal "ownership." This complex relationship means that the taxed land in some instances is under legal jurisdiction of state and county. Legal jurisdiction of trust land is under the Bureau of Indian Affairs and the tribal police. This legal interaction has great implications in regard to the control of inebriants and other policed activities.

Spicer's (1962) analysis of a cultural enclave as "a part of a political society which maintains distinctive cultural traits from the members of the larger whole and which places positive value on the maintenance of these differences" is critical to understanding the dynamics of contemporary reservation communities (265). The sentiments of solidarity or "tribalism" with the in-group as opposed to the outsiders (white) are as pronounced as the boundaries of the enclave. The boundary lines separating Indians and whites are not unrelated to the white prejudice in the off-reservation border towns. Most residents of the border towns have slight knowledge of the reservation and view them, as Washburn (1971) indicates, "as islands of privilege or a refuge for incompetence" (205).

Analogous to the federal agency most responsible on the reservation, the BIA, is its counterpart, the Tribal Council, which is composed of members elected from the various communities. This effort at self-government was established under the Indian Reorganization Act (Wheeler-Howard Act) of 1934. The population size of each community does not determine the number of representatives on the Tribal Council. The elected tribal chairman is administrative head of the tribe with direct powers of veto residing in the agency superintendent of the Bureau of Indian Affairs. In addition to several federal and state agencies, the Tribal Council can be indicated as a native bureaucratic system that mirrors the BIA's functions—Reality, Health, Education, and Welfare on an indigenous level.

What, then, is the quality of life among the reservation populations? Since the Indian Health Service was transferred to the U.S. Public Service in 1955, mortality rates have declined and life expectancy has increased from 60 years in 1950 to 65.1 years in 1970. It is still, however, the lowest of any population group in the United States. Between 1955 and 1971, Indian infant death rates decreased 54 percent and maternal death rates 56 percent. Death from tuberculosis declined 86 percent, gastritis 88 percent, and influenza 57 percent. But health care remains a serious problem. The death rate for Indians from accidents was three times the national average in 1971, as was the mortality rate for cirrhosis of the liver, tuberculosis, and gastritis. There are certain afflictions that continue to affect Indian people in a disproportionate manner. Between 1965 and 1971, the incidence of otitis media (a disease of the inner ear) increased by 74 percent. Strep throat and scarlet fever increased, as did influenza. High rates of alcoholism are still prevalent among many Indian tribes (American Indian Policy Review Commission 1977, 91).

In the 1960s, housing for Indians improved owing to considerable aid from the Housing and Urban Development federal agency. These programs placed housing in communities by concentrating the scattered families that had previously been placed on allotments. The allotment system originally gave 160 acres to each male head of household. Among the Sioux, this new settlement pattern weakened the traditional kin unit, the extended family (*tiospaye*). The recent concentration of unrelated families in communities is a trying experience for many Lakota persons. In addition, increases of populations into towns that previously had not allowed Indian occupancy, for instance McLaughlin, present problems in school attendance, policing, and some intergroup tensions. With supplemental funding from the Indian Education Act, passed in 1972, a swimming pool was built at the local public school; public sentiment against Indian students using the pool necessitated a lawsuit by Indian parents. Yet, this community relies heavily upon Indian trade for its survival.

At present, the average Indian household numbers five occupants, with a transiency of occupants that sometimes exceeds ten. On Standing Rock, composite households are composed of kin (and often nonkin), and larger households are the rule. It is not unusual to find six to ten people residing in the newer housing on the reservation. Unfortunately, this type of introduced dwelling may now be classified as rural slum housing.

Pooling of resources is common on this reservation, and it seems to be a continuation of the sharing ethic. This type of resource management is also characteristic of poverty-stricken households among blacks (Stack 1974). Among Lakota Sioux families, the sharing of incomes—including Aid to Families with Dependent Children (AFDC), Old Age Assistance, "lease money" (money obtained from land rental), wages, products of the hunt, and any welfare payments—are contributed in a pattern of reciprocity. This manner of cooperation has long been an adaptive mechanism among this group of Indians.

The social situation as far as economics, community and governmental structure, educational institutions, religious life, and means of communication (English and Lakota or Dakota) are common to all the Teton (Western) Sioux reservations. There has been a great deal of intermarriage, with movement from one's natal reservation to another. Therefore, the information from all previous studies that have dealt with the use of alcohol on one reservation can be extended to others.

Common denominators for all Sioux reservations are their low socioeconomic status, their lack of job opportunities, and a general malaise, which has been interpreted as apathy. The reservations' status as administered enclaves of indigenous peoples and its peoples' powerless subordination are characteristics that underlay Lakota life.

"Everyone Drinks!"
Drinking Behavior among
Contemporary Lakota (Sioux) Indians

5

W E CAN NOW PROCEED to the 1980s situation among the Teton Sioux, joining information on the use of alcohol as it impinges upon the lives of contemporary peoples, with the ethnohistorical background already developed. With a comprehensive background, continuing drinking styles assume more meaning. Many researchers (Hurt and Brown 1965; Maynard 1969; Medicine 1969; Mindell 1968; Whittaker 1961, 1963; and others) point to the predominance of problems attributed to alcohol use among the Lakota and Dakota peoples. This chapter attempts to place native drinking styles into a context that explains the "learning-to-drink" syndrome. It also enlarges the ambiance of alcohol use among the Lakota Sioux and is descriptive of the social situations from which a person who seeks sobriety must extricate oneself. Among the published research findings concerning alcohol use—past and present—assessment will be made here only of those studies that are pertinent to the Standing Rock Sioux.

Previous research suggests that the use of alcohol by American Indians is a complex phenomenon (Carpenter 1959; Devereux 1948; Lemert 1954, 1956a, 1956b, 1958). Comparisons on a cross-cultural basis are important, nonetheless, for these studies have indicated that among tribes where frequent drunkenness is reported, patterns of heavy drinking may be associated with anxiety. Horton (1943) postulates that nonsobriety was related to aspects of acculturation and subsistence. Acculturation has been used to describe drinking habits of all Indians: Graves (1970) for the Navajo, Curley (1967) for the Mescalero Apache, and Littman (1970) for urban Indians are but a few examples.

Assumptions and Indian Drinking

I have previously stressed an underlying belief that suggests the image of the "drunken Indian" is all encompassing and permeates the very fabric of American society. This image building has had a great impact on North American natives who possibly accept the model and act accordingly (Lurie 1971, 1972). Thus, Indians who participate, however marginally, in the larger society's values may also see drunken behavior as normative. Concerning the impact of such labeling, Levy and Kunitz (1974) write:

> The effects of such "labeling" may be extensive and may make a large contribution to the personal disintegration so often commented upon. Nevertheless, the question that remains to be answered is whether this type of Indian drinking because it is expected of him is the only way that he is permitted to behave and whether, it is established that his drinking is anomic, it came to be so only after he was labeled as a drunken Indian. (191)

The entire question of indigenous drinking patterns has achieved a self-fulfilling prophecy as indicated in such works as MacAndrew and Edgerton (1969) and Lurie (1971, 1972). Lurie's initial formulation was criticized by Deloria (1970), who objected to the idea that Indian drinking is a search for identity. Lurie's (1972) later statement indicating that a distinctive Indian drinking style might be a symbolic gesture and defiant act, not only to whites, has some merit. Certainly, among the Lakota Sioux, it is evidenced by a dynamic pattern that suggests a certain group solidarity and, thereby, ethnic identity.

Present-Day Siouan Drinking Patterns

Important, at least from the viewpoint of awareness of an impending problem, the Standing Rock Tribal Council commissioned an early study concerning alcohol use in the late 1950s that was conducted by Whittaker (1961, 1962, 1963, 1966). An innovation in this study was the use of native interviewers. Most of the data describes the situation as it was in 1955, only two years after the repeal of prohibition for Indians. Using a sample of 208 persons from a total listed as 3,037 residents, Whittaker (1962) indicated the incidence of drinking:

> Approximately 70 percent of the Indian population reported that they consume alcoholic beverages, compared to roughly 59 percent of the white comparison population. By sex, 82 percent of the Indian males indicate they drink, compared to 68 percent of the white males; and 55 percent of the Indian females drink, compared with 50 percent of the white

females. Of the Indian females, 71 percent reported that most of their friends drink, and we suspect that the frequency of drinking among these women is higher than the 55 percent reported. (471)

The comparison group was a white population in Iowa (Mulford and Miller 1960). None of the studies on Indian alcohol used in any tribal group has used a nearby white sample for comparative purposes. This, I feel, is a major flaw.

As far as the intensity of imbibing is concerned, Whittaker's (1962) information shows that the incidence of drinking peaks for Sioux males from the age of twenty to twenty-nine, with 99 percent of them drinking. For the females, 72 percent report drinking. "In the 30–39 age group, however, the incidence rose to 85 percent, while among the males, it has declined to 93 percent" (472). He notes that for women drinking declines after age forty.

In the age bracket of fifteen to seventeen years, 50 percent reported drinking, including 60 percent of the boys and 40 percent of the girls. The average age to begin drinking was fifteen and a half, with an intensity range from seventeen to nineteen years. These are startling figures and appear to have continued, based upon my observations from 1967 to 1979.

However, in Whittaker's sample 31 percent abstained, 45 percent drank only occasionally, and 24 percent regularly imbibed. Occasional drinking was designated as fewer than three times per week, while regular drinking was deemed to be three to more times a week. Lack of money was given as one reason for not drinking regularly. Of greater significance was the fact that 45 percent of women were abstainers, but less than a fifth (18 percent) did not drink at all. As for the actual dynamics of consumption patterns, little information is given, except that "Regardless of what he drinks, the Indian tends to consume a large quantity of it at each drinking occasion" (Whittaker 1962, 474). In a concluding summation based upon percentages, Whittaker (1962) states,

> Symptoms of alcoholism and problem drinking were numerous in the sample, although it is recognized that some of these signs may not have the same meaning in the Indian culture as among whites. Of the Indians, 44 percent indicated usually drinking until drunk; 68 percent had been arrested for drunkenness, 35 percent two or more times, 42 percent had experienced blackouts, 25 percent of the latter with increasing frequency; 14 percent had either been hospitalized or had sought medical advice for a body ailment due to drinking; and 9 percent had had delirium tremens. Sprees or binges, ranging in frequency from less than four a year to once a

week, and in duration from 2 to 7 days or more, were reported by more than half of those who drink. (478)

The signs of binge drinking as described by Whittaker are not truly different from those given for other former band-type organized groups such as the Mescalero Apache. Curley (1967) refers to this alcohol consumption pattern as "blitz" drinking, and he adds that the Apache "does not stop drinking until he is intoxicated or has nothing left to drink" (121). Moreover, binge drinking, commonly referred to as a "spree" among the Lakota, appears to be a shared phenomenon among many Indian drinkers (Devereux 1948; Lemert 1958; Levy and Kunitz 1969). It is clearly noted that liquor consumption increased with more money available among the Standing Rock Sioux (Whittaker 1962). Maynard (1969) and Mindell (1968) corroborate these findings with data from Pine Ridge Reservation.

A general pattern exists throughout the Sioux reservations. There are specific times when liquor flows. These are on paydays, at times when lease checks are sent to landowners, and when money from land sales are received. My data are reinforced by Kemnitzer (1972). The "first of the month" signifies a more regular fund dispersal. Money from welfare, Aid to Dependent Children, and Social Security ("old age" payments) are received. The sharing ethic prevails, and these windfalls often herald a time for drunken revelry and subsequent misfortunes—fights, arrests, and marital/liaison discord. These are the times when binge or spree (or in Siouan *itomani* or drunken) behavior occurs. It is the time also when the Lakota people are more visible in the border towns contiguous to the reservations where most of them shop for groceries, clothing, and other services. In the summer months, white townspeople in these towns often drive to, and park outside, the ubiquitous "Indian bar" in the least desirable part of the town's business district to "watch Indians." Their image of the "drunken, worthless Indian" is thus reinforced.

It is also during this time, and on subsequent weekends, that white farmers and ranchers obtain cheap labor for harvesting and ranching chores. On most Sunday mornings, one can observe farmers and ranchers paying the drunk and disorderly fines for Lakota males, who then labor for them until the jail fine is paid. Ironically, very often the male Lakota may be one of the heirs of the land leased by the white land operator. Jorgenson (1971) illustrates this practice among the Northern Utes: "If an Indian male is jailed in town for drunkenness, his fine of from $15 to $30 is often paid by a local rancher. In turn, the Indian must work for a week or two in the white man's hay field, which is often leased from Indians" (108). The

Dawes Allotment Act of 1887 granted individual ownership of tribal lands by assigning 160 acres of land to every male household head. Most of the original allotments are now fractionated. Individual interests in land can commonly be as minuscule as a one-sixty-fourth heirship, or less. This, of course, again reflects the value of sharing as a cultural imperative for the Lakota. Land is left to the entire *tiospaye* (extended family) with the resultant heirship problem of numerous owners. Leasing the land is often the only alternative for income. The small amounts of money paid at "lease time" are the only source of income for many Sioux people.

Whatever the source of income, Lakota imagery of drinking is quite different from non-Indians. English terms as well as Siouan descriptions are used as markers. The term "alcoholism" is seldom used on the reservation. However, "alcoholic" is often used to describe any Lakota person who drinks. This term is in the forefront when interacting with health personnel or Lakota individuals engaged in alcoholism programs. The term "alcoholic" has come into prominence since the 1960s and reflects the jargon of the "alcoholic workers," as the health personnel are often called. This term refers also to those persons of Lakota ancestry who work in governmental or tribal treatment programs. When pressed for a definition of alcoholism, most Lakota persons replied that it was "when you have to use it everyday" or "when you have to get a drink everyday." However, it is virtually impossible, because of economic and transportation factors, for any Lakota to "use it everyday." This raises the issue of the occurrence of alcoholism in native communities. Alcoholism, alcohol addiction, and alcohol dependence have been reported differently by persons studying alcohol use among Indians (Kemnitzer 1972; Maynard 1969; Mindell 1968), and specifically for the Lakota Sioux. Leland (1976) presents a cogent argument that terms have not been standardized, nor are they of much utility in defining American Indian drinking styles. She writes:

> Many observers of Indian drinking apparently are unaware that "alcoholic addiction" is not a well-defined phenomenon and that there is little agreement as to what manifestations constitute valid indicators of the diagnostic category. The alcohol literature is very large and scattered. Most people who have not consulted this literature hold the "commonsense" conviction that everybody knows an "alcohol addict" when they see one. (126)

Although Mindell (1967) indicates that in his judgment there were alcoholics at Pine Ridge, and Whittaker (1962, 478) states that "symptoms of alcoholism and problem drinking were numerous in the sample" of 208 subjects on Standing Rock Reservation, this writer would prefer not to indulge in the definition of alcoholism. The fact that alcohol is seen as a debilitating feature in contemporary life among the Lakota seems to be a sufficient rationale to investigate how and why persons achieve sobriety by "leaving it alone," as the Lakota say.

Whittaker, it seems, was cognizant of the different styles of drinking exhibited among Indians and non-Indians, but he did not explicitly outline these. He notes in his second article that "the causes of heavy drinking and alcoholism among the Standing Rock Sioux are numerous and complex" (1963, 86). He attributes the high incidence of alcohol consumption to intrapsychic stress, cultural disorganization, and lack of social controls against drinking (Whittaker 1966).

Since his baseline study, there have been other studies from reservations where Lakota people reside. Mohatt (1972) suggests that the drinking of alcohol imparts an aspect of power to male participants and possibly fleeting respect from their peer group. The result is enhanced self-esteem. Using four male case studies, Mohatt reconstructed the pattern of drinking among males on the Rosebud Reservation, where the objective of drinking is to get intoxicated. The pattern noted in other studies (Kemnitzer 1972; Maynard 1969; Whittaker 1963) was confirmed. Because intoxication was the expected goal, the sharing of any and all inebriating beverages was required. Not to share violated the basic tenet of Lakota society— generosity. It is the most compelling and ongoing of the four cardinal virtues of the Lakota people. MacGregor (1945) lists the others as bravery, fortitude, and moral integrity (106–7). Generosity is the most important character trait instilled in Lakota children in the socialization process. Children are taught that "if you don't have anything to feed a visitor, at least give them a drink of water." Stinginess is abhorred in Lakota society. Saving or "being tight," as it is called, is looked upon as "being like a white person." This description is used as a powerful tool for conformity toward a cultural mandate of giving. Therefore, the offering of food, alcoholic beverages, or any other item is a normative act in Lakota culture.

The sharing syndrome, called "setting up," in reservation English, is important and mandatory in the distribution of intoxicants to any and all, of either sex and any age, who may be present when a drinking session begins. To refuse a drink is tantamount to giving a slap in the face. When one does not accept, one is accused of "being too good to drink with us," or as being "not like a Lakota." In such an egalitarian ambience, one must always behave in a way that gives one credence and recognition as being a good Lakota, *Lakota K'tcha*, or the ultimate Lakota person.

Maynard (1969), an anthropologist who spent many years working on Pine Ridge Reservation, notes:

> Reactions to drinking vary but from observations it can be said that drinking releases inhibitions: the non-communicative become loquacious, the quiet raucous and/or aggressive. Insults are heard which would not be permitted in a state of sobriety. Wife beating which rarely occurs when a man is sober is not uncommon when in a state of intoxication. Most acts of physical aggression that result in wounds or even death occur while a person is under the influence of liquor. (39)

Prager (1972) writes about the situation he observed as a medical doctor on the Cheyenne River Reservation:

> They are strangely silent. . . . This Indian passivity and silence, however, is deceptive. Mild alcoholic intoxication is all that is needed to allow the seething, repressed hatred and frustration to surface. Unfortunately for the Indians (fortunately for the white man) these hatreds, once unleashed by alcohol, are directed inwardly and towards members of the immediate family. Wife beatings by intoxicated husbands are common. Recurrent episodes of wild drunken driving, leading to serious injury and death, represent this prevalent self-destructive tendency of the Sioux. In the younger age groups, especially among the dormitory students, suicidal gestures, breath holding contests, glue sniffing, and self-laceration are common. Only rarely, on the other hand, are epithets hurled at white people; even rarer are instances of Indian attacks on whites. (23)

These descriptions are still valid in varying degrees on the Standing Rock and other Lakota Sioux Reservations. Drinking alcohol with resultant intoxication and deviant behavior may be seen as a way of life—a way of coping with the dismal socioeconomic conditions on these reservations. One often hears persons say, "Everyone drinks now," or "I can't criticize them, because I drink, too."

There is tremendous pressure from peers to drink alcohol. This is especially so for Lakota males to whom drinking means becoming or being masculine. Most males drink to demonstrate their *bloka* "character." *Bloka* can be translated from Siouan to correspond to the Spanish *macho* or chauvinistic behavior. However, a more appropriate English gloss is male superiority, a desirable character trait among Lakota males. This is especially significant in opposition to the term *winkte*, which not only means womanlike but also commonly designates a male homosexual. In a culture that previously institutionalized male homosexuality, the term is now generally colored with ridicule and derision. Manhood is signaled by *bloka*-ness, and current enactment of masculinity is demonstration of the ability to drink. For a Lakota male to refuse a drink is a sign of weakness and femininity and often results in teasing and verbal abuse. The connotation of a dare is important here. One often hears male teenagers being dared to "Be a man! Have a drink!" All indications and inclinations are that it is normative for a Sioux male to drink alcohol. It is a sign of manhood and maturity. It is also based on the traditional valuation of Lakota males and the special care and love lavished upon them by all members of the *tiospaye*, and more especially, the mothers. More so for males, individual autonomy is stressed, and censure for deviant acts is not strongly exerted.

There is, then, a definite pattern to drunken Lakota masculine behavior. It begins by drinking a great deal of any available alcoholic beverage. This is the feeling good stage in which talking, joking, and bragging—the telling of tales of daring and success—occurs. This is often referred to as a "laughing spell" by some males (Mohatt 1972, 274). It is followed by a period of maudlin reminiscences that often leads to tears. This is one of the few times when Sioux males resort to tears in public. This phase can be traumatic for young children who may be present. After this comes a stage in which bellicosity and belligerence dominate. Kuttner and Lorincz (1967) indicate that drunkenness allows Sioux individuals to display aggressiveness that is under control when they are sober. This aggressive behavior often results in fights and acts of violence. The final state is complete comatoseness—called "passing out" by the Lakota in reservation vernacular. This stage—passing to an ultimate state of stupor—does not exactly correspond to Kemnitzer's (1972) states of drunkenness. His documentation of drunken states at Pine Ridge sequences them as follows: "initiating a party," "first animation," "slightly high," "tipsy," "happy," "depression," and then "indignation and fights" (139–40).

The Lakota themselves do not have such elaborate distinctions, but certain stages of inebriation can be defined. The linguistic domain shows the differences in indigenous perceptions of the drunken states. These sociolinguistic categories describe various stages of drunkenness. Jules-Rosette (1978) posits that descriptive vocabularies "both alter the experience through indexing it and are transformed by the experience" (570). The description is especially apt when the vocabularies of both Lakota and English are juxtaposed to delineate stages of inebriation. Native terms were elicited from Lakota persons. These taxonomic categories were agreed upon to correspond with English utterances.

In the literature of bilingual education, vernacular English is often referred to as Reservation English, Indian English, or Red English. Native languages are often called "Indian" by native peoples themselves; thus, one hears the phrase "speaking Indian." Native Sioux referential terminology is different from the white mode when they discuss drinking among themselves. The term "alcoholic" is a term borrowed from the health practitioners on the reservations and is used to describe anyone who drinks. To any other person who drinks occasionally, it is usually stated "he or she drinks," or in Lakota "yat ka' un" (he, she, it drinks). Or if a person drinks alcohol frequently, one says in Lakota that "iyo mani s'a" or "that person gets drunk." In Lakota perspective, the English term "alcoholic" refers to one who purchases alcohol when money is available and then becomes drunk. This pattern is usual and predictable. It is difficult for nonresidents to realize the impoverished conditions on most reservations in the Sioux area. The general lack of money makes continual drinking impossible. This fact is pertinent to the binge-drinking syndrome. It is also significant that spree drinking may be a protective or adaptive feature. The sporadic nature of drinking at least allows Lakota persons to maintain regular nutrition programs and apparently does not foster alcohol-related malnutrition. Cause of death among Lakota persons is often diagnosed as cirrhosis of the liver. The vernacular is simply "cirrhosis" or in Lakota *pxe-shica* or "bad liver" (see table 5.1).

The foregoing presentation of native terms is not merely a catalog of utterances that add an ethnoscientific approach to the Lakota consciousness-altering experiences of inebriation. Altered states have significance for the participants. Their terms are not only descriptive, but they also reflect expectations that are grounded in their particular culture. They express shared knowledge, which indicates categories of drinking states, possible varieties of drinkers, but more importantly, from an intervention mode, they express behaviors indicative of stages of drunkenness. Sharpened explications of behavioral norms for tribal groups focus upon behaviors that can be classed as normative or deviant. As Whittaker's studies (1962, 1963) indicate, the Standing Rock Sioux exhibited little knowledge about the contours of alcohol use and its effects, that is, effects of prolonged drinking or cirrhosis. By utilizing cognitive systems, prevention programs might be more efficacious. Cognitive systems in tandem with the stringent delineation of contextual cultural behaviors examined systematically are more effective in assessing "drunken comportment." More significantly, the two-partite cognitive frame symbolizes well the dual world in which Lakota persons interact in contemporary society. Indulgence in alcohol may be a mediating factor.

Table 5.1.   Linguistic Chart

Standard English	Vernacular English	Lakota Dialect Siouan
Nonintoxicated	Sober	*Ito mani shni* (Drunk not); *T'yan ahbles ya nhan* (Composure having or examining carefully)
Slightly intoxicated	Getting Tight, Getting greased, Feeling good, Getting high	*Ahg'a* or *Ni slo he? Kitanla o waste' ka* (Wavering, uncertainly; slightly exhilarated; in good shape)
Intoxicated	Drunk, Gone, Polluted	*Ito mani** or *Ito kes ke omani* (In an unusual way, walking; at present, these translations are given: to stagger, reeling, spinning, and to get dizzy); *Tuktel iya ye* (Where gone is unclear); *Ti yes ni* (Not at home)
Comatose	Passed out, Dead drunk	*O t'e* (Dead); *O t'e xpi ya* (Deadly sleep); *O t'e ito mani* (Dead drunk)
Delirium tremens	The shakes, D.T.s	*Chan chan un* (Shaking, in state of)
Hallucinations	Seeing snakes	*Skan skan wa yanke* (Moving things are seen); *Zuzecha wayanke* (Snakes are seen); *Taku t'ok t'okcha wa yanke* (Strange things are seen)

*Riggs (1851) translates *i-to'-ho-mni-* as an adjective, "dizzy, light headed, drunk" (96). *Ito mani* is a contracted form of the previous term.

Most observers of and writers about drinking styles among the Lakota note that the aim of drinking is to get drunk as soon and as quickly as possible (Kemnitzer 1972; Maynard 1969; Mohatt 1972). Some have noted the social setting in which drinking behavior is learned. Kemnitzer (1972), basing his perceptions on Pine Ridge, gives the following description, which is relevant to all the Sioux reservations:

> Although the main environments for social drinking are homes, car parks, and bars, in all of these the whole family is included. Small children are present at drinking parties, and infants are taken to bars and there suckled, or beer and wine is mixed in their bottles. Children under twelve play around the drinkers in bars, and by the age of fifteen are in drinking groups of their own, but do not participate in public bar drinking until they are older. Adolescents are also sniffing gasoline and glue as well as drinking alcoholic beverages. The drinking culture is also expressed in the play of younger children:

Two young boys are playing with toy cars. They pretend to load the cars with people, drive the car to White Clay for wine, get drunk, and wreck the cars on the way home. Little girls playing with dolls make up a situation where the "parents" get drunk and fight.

Young children are also coerced by older children and adolescents to sniff gasoline and to drink. Thus, values and behavior reinforcing traditional drinking patterns are transmitted by example and instruction to children of all ages, and drunken behavior becomes "normal" behavior for a significant segment of the population. (139)

That the "significant segment of the population" is not specified does not negate the fact that the patterns of participation in drinking behavior are well established by the time the child becomes an adolescent and a member of a peer group. This is important in the continuation of drinking styles. This "training" for alcohol consumption was noted on Standing Rock from 1967 to 1979.

This conditioned propensity for alcohol consumption is carried into the nexus of the reservation and border town. In describing the "culture of excitement" for the Sioux, White (1970) indicates a "folkway":

For the Sioux Indian one of the most important is chronic drinking to excess. This is the easiest way to quick elation and excitement, a way to relax and forget the fears and insecurities of one's life. It is also a means for the Sioux, who by tradition is dignified and reserved, to be loud, raucous, and cocky in his repartee. In his elation, he forgets any sense of inferiority and gains a feeling of power and assurance—ready to accept any dare. (189)

White's categorization of folkways, which characterized the "culture of excitement," could well be correlated with the culture of poverty. He includes such norms as the "readiness for physical violence," "violation of the law or vandalism," and "sex play." He states that the culture he describes is "shared by men and women of all age groups" (190). He continues: "Sioux lower-class subgroup with its focal point in the line of bars on Rapid City's Main Street tends to be a world apart even from the rest of the Indian community" (189). His description fits a type of urban nomadism (Spradley 1970) and Indian drinking behavior in urban areas as seen in "Indian bars."

Hurt and Brown (1965) have noted that the patterns of alcohol consumption have become solidified since the Eastern Dakota began using alcohol. Their study of the urban Dakota, an eastern group in South Dakota, indicates that excessive drinking was not atypical of drinkers in the early period. However, as this group became urbanized, a noticeable increase in the consumption pattern was observable. It appears that intensified contact with white communities fostered alcohol use among the Eastern and Western Siouan groups. Before the final stage of drinking to satiation and stupor, most writers agree with Kuttner and Lorincz (1967) that drunkenness allows Sioux individuals, especially males, to display aggressive comportment that is under control in a state of sobriety. My observations support these descriptions.

There is little in the literature on alcohol concerning the topic of the drinking styles of Indian women. Leland (1978) has noted the utilization of alcohol as a coping strategy for Indian women in Nevada. Maynard (1969) again supplies some observations from Pine Ridge Reservation:

> In the case of the women, the attitude is quite different. In some situations and among some groups women are also under pressure to drink. In general, however, the woman who does not drink is respected and the woman who drinks is criticized. Especially open to censure are women who neglect their children because of drinking or who hang around the bars unescorted. (40)

This aptly describes current views on Standing Rock.

White (1970) indicates that, in the Rapid City group, both men and women were "equally ready to fight physically" (189). Moreover, women apparently operated in the subgroup's sexual code that was not explicated except that "at the bottom of the group (in status as well as the meaning of life) are women who have become prostitutes and the complete derelicts known on Main Street as the 'winos'" (192). He indicates that the men stationed at the air base, cowboys coming into the city, and traveling construction workers often become "friends" who support some Indian women as long as they are in the area. An important consideration in the relationships between Lakota males and females is the pressure of the peer group for the male to continue in his drinking pattern. This often leads to a dissolution of the marriage—legal or consensual—and the woman's dependence on Aid to Dependent Children. Very often, single Lakota women after a marriage failure gravitate to a life on the "Main Streets" of the northern Plains communities.

It is possible to discern a pattern in Lakota female drinking behavior. Whittaker (1962) notes that, in contrast to males, women on Standing Rock Reservation showed a lesser tendency to drink large amounts of liquor at a single sitting. However, he also notes that they consumed a larger amount than the white sample population in Iowa. Speaking within a time frame of the 1950s, he delineates a pattern of generational differences among Indian women, stating, "of the female respondents, 55 percent drink, compared to 20 percent of their mothers" (477). The increase of drinking among Lakota women appeared to be accelerating at the time of my fieldwork in the 1970s. Whittaker also notes that women tended to stop drinking when children were born. This was not evident to me. I was, however, unable to find any evidence of fetal alcohol syndrome. Scrutiny of records of the Indian Health Service was not allowed during the study. Characteristics of 1970s drinking patterns on most of the Lakota Sioux reservations present a change from the previous decade (Hurt and Brown 1965; Kemnitzer 1972; Maynard 1969; Medicine 1969; Mohatt 1972) in that an overall increase is evident. This is verified by Whittaker's follow-up study (1982).

My data indicate that from 1960 onward, drinking by females during childbearing age became more frequent. Women's responses to their husbands' continued "boozing" is to join them. This is more usual than one imagines. Many Lakota women verbalize this actual behavior when they say, "If you can't lick them, join them." After pleading for years for abstinence, or at least sporadic drinking on the part of their husbands, they accompany the men to bars and begin to drink. For some, this is only a transitory action. They stop when they have convinced their husbands to lessen their alcohol consumption. For other Sioux women, drinking becomes a way of life. Then there are some Sioux women, as with Indian women of other tribes (Leland 1978), who are able to go into a bar or restaurant and "drink like whites." In border towns off the reservation, this means that they might have a cocktail or beer before a meal or go to a local bar where live music is featured. Others do not go to bars or drink at all. These are often older women or those who have achieved sobriety.

Lakota women have always been aware of alcohol use, even before it became legal. Some from families who were *o ki se'* (literally, "halves," or "half-breeds" as they are called in reservation English) saw their father drinking liquor. Some of these Lakota fathers, because of phenotypic structures of their appearances, could purchase liquor. Some were bootleggers. If a father was a white man, frequently he might purchase liquor for his Indian friends and relatives.

Many of the young women who grew to adulthood just after the lifting of the ban on alcohol consumption in 1953 learned to drink as part of their adolescent experience. As for males, learning to drink is almost a puberty rite. Introduction to alcohol use becomes a part of the growing up process for both sexes. The gradual indoctrination to alcohol consumption is accomplished in several ways. Generally, a female learns drinking behavior in the family setting. In most cases her father and mother are drinkers, and her initiation into drinking is not a problem to them. Many families actively encourage young daughters to accompany them on drinking bouts. Others carefully guard their daughters from peer group interaction; the number in this category has steadily declined since the decade of the 1950s.

Families who encourage daughters, or do not discourage them, to participate in drinking are fatalistic. The girl will drink no matter what they do. The daughter who drinks may become a form of insurance as a source for alcoholic beverages. She can recruit white ranchers, farmers, and even police officials to support the drinking habit she acquires. Her extended kin, if composed of heavy drinkers, share in this symbiotic relationship. The evoking of Lakota "setting up" guarantees supply. Indian women who fit this description very often form liaisons (sometimes sexual) with bar owners, bartenders, and businessmen to guarantee a source of liquor. Such relationships may become their means of livelihood. The survival strategies of Indian women "winos" and the transient lone Indian man have not been examined in studies of the contemporary lifestyles of Indians of any tribe.

Deviant behavior is not looked down upon by most Lakota people. Derision is not part of their attitude. Statements such as, "Poor thing! He/She can't help it" are often heard. Pity frequently prevails. This is but one example of ineffective normative social control, and it is not unique to Standing Rock Reservation. In describing a town in eastern South Dakota, Hurt (1961) writes:

> A further characteristic of the Indian in Yankton is the numerical superiority of women (141 women and 121 men). Since the sexes are almost equal in number under the age of 18, women are more numerous in the adult group. Men are apparently more transient, leaving Yankton for larger industrial areas, moving back to the reservation, or simply wandering along the open highways. The women are less mobile because their responsible sex role involves care of large numbers of children usually found in the urban Indian family. (227)

Defining the social milieu, he further states, "Unless an Indian is mixed-blood, he has little social contact with the white man except for members of the lowest socioeconomic class. In particular, contacts between young Indian girls and older white men are fairly frequent in bars and in automobiles" (227).

One strand of traditional male and female sibling behavior is illustrative. The institutionalized *hakataku* (meaning "to follow after them") is the expected behavior for a Lakota female's "brothers"—biological and sociological. They are expected to serve as her guardians—"watching and protecting her from other men" (Hassrick 1961, 123). I note that this seemingly anachronistic custom is still apparent in some of the more traditional families. It certainly is not as prominent as it was from the early reservation period until the late 1950s for the majority of "full blood" *tiospaye* (extended families). This is only one example of the breakdown of social structural institutions and the resultant change in a people's interaction pattern. It also represents an acculturational or learning process in which new norms and values were not realistically represented nor internalized in the new socialization systems of educational institutions and religious superstructures that followed the suppression of native belief systems.

In summary, Lakota women fulfill a variety of roles in the nexus of alcohol and everyday living. Some women are willing participants in the drinking game. Others have been compelled to join in—hoping to salvage a marriage or hold a man's attention. Others serve in the capacity of caretakers—driving "the drunks" home, feeding them, cleaning them, and in many other ways helping them through their drunken escapades. Some women act as intercessors or mediators in the interethnic encounters in the off-reservation towns bordering the Indian enclaves. Women—wives, mothers, sisters, aunts, cousins—appear with bail money, plead with non-Indian judges, contact lawyers, and maneuver to keep the Lakota males out of jail. There have been instances in which sexual favors have been granted by women to law officers. The fact that a cultural bias exists in the judicial system is recognized by all—Indians and whites. This is reflected in the common request expressed by Lakota males when they plead with the women of their *tiospaye* to intercede in the legal system. "They listen to you," they say. This and other attitudes have had effects upon role discrepancies and have further implication for the undermining of masculine roles.

Male Drinking Patterns

The most common response to "Why do you drink?" by Lakota males is "Everyone does it." Peer pressure is great and markedly clear during the adolescent period. It carries into the adult years with a residual configuration of the friendship group (*kola*-hood) continuing. The traditional friendship group has become a "drinking buddy" sodality. Previously, indications of the tensions in marriage or liaison relationships were manifested in the pulls toward peer group continuity rather than a stable marriage. The swing of Lakota males to comradeship acceptance is frequently a result of the frustration and failure to obtain jobs to provide a livelihood for their

families. To self-actualize and achieve as well as meet the continual expectation of the larger kin group—the *tiospaye*—to be provided for are difficult demands to fulfill in many contemporary communities. The need to
"pull one's weight," as the Lakota say, in a social structure in which the survival of the unit depends upon equitable contributions of goods, time, and
effort, is a heavy burden. Being unable to provide strikes at the very core
of *bloka*-ness (Lakota masculinity). The social interactions in the family unit
provide a nexus for comprehending the drinking behavior of Lakota males.

Drinking proclivities of Sioux males have been graphically described in
the literature. Blakeslee (1955) refers to "several Dakota males of different
ages and degrees of acculturation" who engage in "riotous eating and
drinking which took place the first two weeks after the arrival of the subsistence check. The end of the month was sober and lean." He notes also
that although the "older men frowned on drunkenness, all opposition to
drinking behavior was passive" (32). His study indicates that more whites
had comments than Indians about drinking behavior; it is difficult to discern the validity of this description. Moreover, he is referring to the Crow
Creek Reservation of Dakota people. The above description, whether
sifted through non-Indian eyes or not, nonetheless, gives an overview. It
also gives a statement of the type of research engendered in powerless
communities (Ryan 1971; Valentine 1968).

Again for the eastern groups, Hurt (1961) writes:

> "Alcoholism" is a problem that plagues Indians in Yankton as it does most
> other North American Indian groups. In one way or another, it is tied to
> a wide variety of crimes and misdemeanors. Thus, in the five-year period
> before 1959, there were 471 arrests for public intoxication with one indi-
> vidual being arrested 39 times and four people over 20 times. In addition,
> there were 71 arrests for disturbing the peace, 27 for assault and battery,
> and 37 for reckless driving, nearly all while intoxicated. It is a mistake to
> label all Indians in Yankton as "alcoholics" even though many are heavy
> drinkers. Excessive use of alcohol is related both to a lack of organized so-
> cial activities and recreation for Indians in the city, and to the fact that In-
> dians have placed a high prestige value on social drinking. Social drinking
> plays such an important role in their lives that the informally organized
> "drinking clubs" are a major unit of local Indian social organization. (228)

Stewart (1964), in a much-quoted national study of Indian criminality,
notes that 71 percent of Indian arrests reported in 1960 were alcohol related. Wax (1971) found that in South Dakota one third of the prison population was Indian as compared to 5 percent of the state's total population.

The picture presented above indicates the harsh reality of the cultural milieu in which Lakota males must operate.

Among Lakota males, drinking alcoholic beverages and participating in the daring exploits that follow are a validation of manhood. This is *bloka* used as a modus operandi for all Lakota males—whether they are fully bilingual or not. *Bloka* means manhood to Lakota males. The "warrior syndrome" has been explicated in ethnographic monographs (Hassrick 1961; MacGregor 1945; Provinse 1937; among others). This valuation of males continues. Its configuration has not been completely assessed within the continuity of cultural ideals. *Bloka* and the "warrior" syndrome are powerful sanctions at play among the Lakota males. The value placed on males is evident. For example, a Lakota female is not fully recognized as a mature woman until she has produced a son. Males feel inadequate, also, until they have fathered a son. A very decided male bias is part of the socialization processes of both male and female children.

In discussing the "culture of excitement," White (1970) gives a slight indication of the androcentric bias when he states, "Within the strictly matriarchal Sioux family the relationship of the mother to the boys is observed to be unusually salient, while in the boys there is frequently a dislike, even a contempt for the absent father or the present but worthless father" (193). In discussing contemporary Lakota family dynamics, I have argued that the qualitative aspects of relationships are somewhat different from the structure of the family (Medicine 1981).

The internalization of the male-centered ideal powerfully motivates young boys, entering adolescence, to drink alcohol. The dare "to prove you're a man" is a powerful incentive to action. It is commonly invoked in peer relationships during a male's maturation process. This daring appears to intensify during puberty, but its acceptance continues throughout a male's lifetime. He must accept it in order to remain a member of the Lakota male peer group—a *kola* group. The native interrogation "ni bloka he?" or "Are you a male?" is a sufficient query to thrust a young or old Lakota male into any feat of daring. Behavior normally exhibited by a Lakota male, provoked by a dare, can range from reckless behavior to self-mutilation attempts—such as withstanding cigarette burns on arms or hands while displaying stoicism and *bloka*-ness. A native utterance such as "Ai! A-tash bloka sni" or "not like a man!" is sufficient to demolish a male Lakota who aspires to be one of the group. Interestingly, a male who resists taunts and dares or exhibits feminine characteristics is often dismissed by being called *winkte*—womanlike or homosexual. There is an awareness that the enactment of the latter role was institutionalized in pre-reservation days by some Sioux people. Others are as merciless in their lack of under-standing as members of the dominant society. Generally, however, a rec-ognized and accepted *winkte* (true homosexual) is not harassed and tempted to drink. English equivalents for *winkte* are "sissies" or "mama's boys"—terms of contempt for those who repeatedly resist the intake of alcoholic beverages. But, since most of the Lakota males wish to be accepted, this cultural ideal of Lakota masculinity very effectively involves men of all ages in the consumption of alcoholic beverages.

One postulate often given is that alcohol is an antidote for frustration and failure (Hurt 1961; Hurt and Brown 1965; Kemnitzer 1972; Maynard 1969). The ability to achieve a steady job is not an easy task in present-day reservation life. Obtaining a job results in a stable income, which in turn al-lows for increased drinking, as Whittaker (1961) has shown. Wages of Lakota males are usually shared—they buy drinks for "drinking buddies" and kin. Drinking to excess then leads to nonperformance or absenteeism from the job, which leads to dismissal and joblessness. The cycle of drunkenness pervades every aspect of Lakota life. Its foundations are built upon reciproc-ity, which guarantees drinking according to the availability of money.

For many Lakota male drinkers, imbibing alcohol may be an acceptable means of dealing with daily frustrations, such as joblessness, marital dis-cord, or stresses within the *tiospaye* where most males live. To many Lakota persons, going to a border town facilitates indulging their taste for alcohol and relieves the boredom and tedium of reservation life. They all have in-dicated that they "drink because there is nothing to do." More frequently, Lakota males say they "like to drink with their buddies." This indicates that their peer group is still a vital part of their lifestyles. White (1970) expli-cates a peer group operation in an off-reservation context. The occasional drunken binge or spree is often the ultimate strategy for dealing with the deeper exigencies of life—divorce, job loss, and in some instances, death of a family member. Lakota have strong taboos regarding behavior after the death of a loved one, with a specific period of mourning. Owing to a fear that *wacunza* (in this case, meaning that "unusual or careless behavior may become habitual") might occur, drinking in this instance is seen as truly deviant and dangerous. The connotation of "imminent justice" that Grob-smith (1974) attributes to the term is not relevant in this context.

Some of the more considerate males, if they are anticipating a binge, may give their wives most of the money they have; others might buy gro-ceries and send these home to their families. Still others might indicate their impending spree in ways that are not so positive, perhaps by provok-ing a quarrel with their wives or antagonizing someone in the kinship group, or by berating a child. This then gives them reasons for a "good drunk," as they say. Some men are able to drink socially with their drinking buddies and leave the group; others stay until the liquor supply or the money ("bank") is exhausted; and others perform all sorts of evasive tactics to avoid a wife, mother, or sister, who may urge them to go home or, indeed, may take them home. Others may become comatose. As they say, "I knocked myself out," to refer to this period of oblivion. This notion comes closest to what MacAndrew and Edgerton (1969) describe as a "time-out" period. Some males, who have reached the penultimate stage of aggression—fighting peer group members, or on daring occasions, "fighting the *washichu*" (white men)—are then subjected to the ultimate phase of drinking—jail. Many Lakota males are finally incarcerated for resisting arrest. Other charges include DWI (driving while intoxicated), drunk and disorderly, assaulting an officer, or having a broken seal. This latter charge means that persons are in a vehicle in which a bottle with a broken seal is found. Any of these violations result in immediate arrest and jail, with resultant fines.

The above pattern of behavior ensures that on Monday morning, or perhaps on Sunday, Lakota wives, mothers, sisters, and girlfriends scurry around to raise bail money to get their men out of jail—especially if the men are working and have to be back on the job on Monday morning.

As for the Lakota women, some of them begin drinking after their men are put in jail. Some of them say, "O kab ble ya ima tomni k' te"—"With ease, or without care, I will get drunk." Thus, drinking has a tension-reduction aspect for Lakota women also. When queried further, many of the women responded, "Well, I know where he is, now!" This is the time when a type of social bonding occurs among Lakota women. Two or three of the women who are attached in some manner—by marriage, consensual marriage, or consanguinity—to the jailed men might "get drunk." Usually, they stay in the border town to mediate between the Lakota males and the law. Lakota males accept this practice because according to them policemen, lawyers, and judges listen to women when pleas are made. One can readily see the impotent dimensions of the power differential in Indian-white male interaction.

In line with this latter aspect, many programs in the various administrations (Bureau of Indian Affairs, U.S. Public Health Service, Housing and Urban Development, and other agencies) have instituted a hiring policy that favors Lakota women, whom they see as more dependable than men. This is one feature of excessive drinking by Indian men that is seldom explored in studies. Many younger Sioux men have made adjustments to being caretakers of young children. This trend is somewhat affected by the opening of day-care centers on some reservations. However, a new status for some Lakota males is not lost on their peer group, and some are teased for being househusbands. An antifeminist movement is strong on some Sioux reservations, with many women who work being labeled as "women's libbers." The trend to the establishment of shelters for battered women and incidences of spouse, parent, and child abuse have risen markedly since 1970. This is a new concern for Lakota communities.

For the Lakota Sioux in general, there are several viewpoints resulting from studies on drinking that seem more relevant than others. Whittaker (1962, 1963) offers a psychodynamic explanation in proposing that the Standing Rock Sioux individuals drank to deal with the uncertainties of reservation life. This interpretation seems valid for that period. Mohatt (1972) delineates the need for personal power among males from Rosebud that underlined the need for drinking alcohol. Lurie (1971) indicates that heavy drinking had repercussions for all Indians, for drinking was an "Indian" thing to do. For her, it was an act that could be interpreted as a self-fulfilling prophecy. If one views Lurie's notion and puts drinking in a situation as a reaction to administered relationships, her thesis attains different dimensions. This interpretation may be implicit in her statement that "getting drunk remains a very Indian thing to do when all else fails to maintain the Indian-white boundary" (325). This would not, however, explain Lakota male aggressive acts against the white males and policemen in many border towns in South Dakota. A more realistic view might be the extension of aggression to an out-group in a more fatalistic way. All Lakota males know that resisting arrest is sure to mean incarceration.

Periodic "binges" certainly have tension-releasing functions for the Lakota, especially males. Frustration, aggression, and out-group bellicosity are met in states of various degrees of inebriation. This does not explain, however, how some Sioux males can run away from the police or when they are outnumbered by *washichu* (white) foes. Previous to the fisticuffs, certain Sioux males almost passed out (comatose) are yet able to flee when outnumbered. Apparently, drinking allows certain adaptation in intergroup relations.

Aspects of domination and submission that are characteristic of reservations today are factors in contemporary Indian life that have not been explored sufficiently. Racist attitudes off the reservations have not been the focus of studies dealing with alcohol use. Levy and Kunitz (1971b) and Levy (1965) suggest that life on reservations with the administered human relationships and control of aspirations for Indian people may be sufficient cause to drink. Elsewhere I have suggested that perhaps the drinking context was an emergent behavioral system that presented a believable reality to most Lakota males (Medicine 1969).

Saslow and Harrover (1968) and, more specifically for the Lakota groups, Kemnitzer (1972) suggest that drinking alcohol as a lifestyle might be attributed to the modeling that occurs on reservations. There is little doubt that parents and parental surrogates in the *tiospaye* offer models and patterns of drinking behavior that are emulated by children. A short report of a study of fifty-one Chippewa males in a treatment facility in Minnesota (Hoffman and Noem 1975) indicates that alcoholism is more prevalent among the relatives of Indian patients than among non-Indian patients, with the percentage of abstaining parents much lower among Indians than non-Indians. This speaks to the socialization process exemplified in play activities noted by Kemnitzer (1972). Further, Hoffman and Noem relate the high incidence of Chippewa male alcohol addiction to frustration and low socioeconomic conditions on the reservations, the stress-related absence of natural parents during childhood, and also to the exposure during childhood to heavily imbibing adults. There is a dearth of socialization studies for contemporary Siouan groups, but the proximity to adult drinkers and opportunity to observe drinking behavior is prevalent. This is a strong factor in attitudes about alcohol. All studies on Lakota drinking habits indicate the strength and continuous operation of the peer group for males (Kemnitzer 1972; Maynard 1969; Mindell 1968; Mohatt 1972; Whittaker 1963). My data suggest that there is a similar peer group for Lakota women when they choose to "go drinking."

Unfortunately, most reports to date have emphasized that many tribal groups accept drinking as normative and, in essence, seem to condone it (Curley 1967; Dozier 1966; Hurt and Brown 1965; Kemnitzer 1972; Kuttner and Lorincz 1967; Lemert 1958). Among the Lakota, it might appear that drinking and deviance (incarceration for drunkenness and aggression, suicide, and homicide indices) are tolerated on reservations where they are generated by the people themselves and may be attributed to such Lakota norms as personal autonomy valuation and a strong feeling that acts committed in a drunken state are more or less excusable. Several legal systems in operation at the same time put social control on a very tenuous base. The fact that there is often a protective shield thrown around the deviant is also a factor for consideration. As has been noted previously, drinking is considered acceptable on many Indian reservations other than Lakota. Braroe (1975) has argued that excessive drinking in which Canadian Cree indulge does not produce a sense of guilt or a violation of self-image. He contends that whites, however, often feel guilty on account of acts of aggression and drunkenness and thus impute this feeling to Indian drinking.

Among the Lakota Sioux, the essence of being is tied up in the kinship bond (Deloria 1945; MacGregor 1945; Mirsky 1937; Schusky 1975), and any evidence of coercion or control by kin is a transgression against the individual. The anachronistic value of sharing is one of the salient features of Lakota life today and is a strong determinant in the drinking style. Older traditional forms of social control were weakly developed. The mechanisms, which took form in *akicita* (soldier) societies, were formulated to meet certain specific needs, such as the regulation of the hunt and the Sun Dance. Aspects of the ritual cycle were completely denied in the early reservation period. This fact, along with the denial of the hunter and warrior roles, rendered the male actualization pattern almost impotent during this time. The *akicita* societies were replaced by agent-appointed police who were called *maku maza* (metal breasts) and were seen as enemies rather than peacekeepers. The name and attitude still apply to the tribal police of today.

Field's (1962) arguments regarding social structural features in the traditional society have relevance. Band-type organizations, such as Apache (Curley 1967; Levy and Kunitz 1974) and the Lakota, have not yet developed tightly structured social control mechanisms that regulate alcohol use and abuse. For the Lakota, at least, a continued emphasis on incorporativeness of kin, no matter what transgression was committed while under the influence of intoxicants, is strong. An ongoing stress upon and valuation of individual autonomy (*chin k'a cha*) are strong factors explaining why and how persons drink. More important, how Sioux persons achieve and maintain sobriety reflects individual autonomy. Much reliance is upon individual willpower to drink or not to drink.

It is my contention that for the Lakota the breaking of social relationships and the transgressions that result from drinking are not irreparable. Individuals who drink are not chastised by the in-group, punished, or made to feel guilty. This characteristic of Lakota life does not serve as a strong social control mechanism. The continued reincorporation of the individual into the kinship group seems to foster the drinking pattern that is established early in one's maturation. Taking this characteristic into account is critical to an understanding of the attempts to achieve sobriety. The individual who strives to attain a changed lifestyle can be certain of alienation from the social group, particularly his peer group of drinking buddies.

That arena of the emergence from dependence upon alcohol will now be examined. Though there is stress on individual autonomy, the pattern of an egalitarian society exists in the present. Sharing is not limited to liquor, however. The giving of food, shelter, clothing, and other essentials contributes to survival on the reservations. The ethic of giving means simply that what is available is utilized by all. This pattern of hospitality, which is evident on the reservations in Sioux country, extends to urban Indians.

Over 60 percent of the Indians in North America live in urban areas. The urbanization process began for the Sioux in the 1950s with the Relocation Program of the Bureau of Indian Affairs. Its goal was to move Indians from impoverished reservations to jobs in the urban areas of Chicago, Minneapolis, Los Angeles, and San Francisco. However, the procedure for many Sioux reservations was to give chronic drunks or habitual occupants of jails the choice of relocation or continued incarceration. Many of the Sioux had already moved to urban areas during World War II. Some of the migrants were nondrinkers and made a good adjustment to urban life. Most drinkers simply moved a reservation problem to an urban context (Graves 1971; Medicine 1973; Price 1968). Studies of Indian urbanization proliferated during the 1960s. In an early study that is often listed in bibliographies on Indian drinking, Ablon (1964) indicates that "each of the major relocation centers has several 'Indian bars' in the central districts where many Indian men and women of a variety of tribes congregate and meet new friends and sexual partners. Others visit bars only on payday, or stop by on Holidays for a few drinks" (298). This is the context in which drinking patterns are seen in contemporary urban centers. Ablon makes a cogent point about the general value orientation of a variety of urban Indians from various tribal groups, stating: "In general all Indians and especially the Sioux tend to feel the responsibility of helping their kinsmen or tribesmen when asked, and will give money, food, or lodging to a needy family" (298). This is meaningful, as it shows the perpetuation of generosity in a new environment.

A summation of my observations of the drinking styles of the Lakota Sioux on Standing Rock Reservation from 1976 to 1980 follow. The number of women involved in alcohol consumption increased after the 1960s. Peer-pressured drinking behavior remained prevalent among Lakota males with earlier experimentation among both males and females. The main periods of drinking were, understandably, still determined by the tie of economic affluence—payday, time of lease dispersals, and "first of the month" payments. However, there is an emerging pattern of drinking that approximates what Lakota characterize as "drinking like whites," although there is also a more regularized pattern, which in some cases is intense. The flamboyance and novelty of the period from the 1950s to the early 1960s is less marked.

In regard to the Standing Rock Reservation, Whittaker (1982) indicates that in "the use of alcohol over the past twenty years, it appears that excessive drinking has stabilized at a chronic high level. . . . Our figures suggest that the overall rate of drinking may have declined somewhat since 1960, but we suspect this is due in large part to the numbers of people abstaining from alcohol use due to severe alcohol-related problems" (32). Nonetheless, I find that the area of self-achieved, continuous sober state remains an undocumented phenomenon that is discussed next.

American Indian Sobriety
An Uncharted Domain

6

SOBRIETY, AS A DISTINCT FEATURE in the behavioral framework of alcohol studies regarding American Indian groups, has not engaged the imagination of researchers. As mentioned earlier, a "social problem" framework has prevailed. This has been important in obtaining funds for ameliorative purposes. A greater comprehension of the dynamics of self-determination in native communities is projected by examining this relatively unknown aspect of Indian drinking. Lakota drinking—at all times and on all occasions—has strong emotional, social, and economic components. What are the actions involved in leaving this state of drinking behavior and reaching a continual and chosen sober state?

Levy, an anthropologist, and Kunitz, a medical doctor and sociologist, spent much time researching Indian use of alcohol among the Navajo, Hopi, and White Mountain Apache, writing:

> First, all of the manifestations of alcoholism have come to our attention through experience with heavy drinkers in our own and other Western societies. There is no guarantee that a similar association will prevail in another culture. Moreover, as the diagnosis must be made on the basis of manifestations, there is no method readily available for testing the validity of the association in other cultures. Secondly, all of the manifestations are, to a greater or lesser degree, culturally defined and determined, especially those used as indicators in most epidemiological investigations. The economic ill effects of drinking are defined and measured by Western standards as are the social effects of broken homes, overt aggression, etc. In an Indian society where divorce was common in aboriginal times, where economic opportunities are limited for drinkers and nondrinkers alike and where arrests are made for breaches of white rather than aboriginal norms

and laws, it is difficult to determine whether these behaviors are caused by drinking, are themselves causes of drinking, or are fortuitously associated due to the fact that all these behaviors occur frequently in many Indian communities.

Most investigators would agree that the more physiologically based indicators like Laennec's cirrhosis or the withdrawal syndrome are less culture bound than are the behavioral manifestations. Yet, it is just such data which have been lacking in virtually all studies of Indian drinking to date. It is not surprising then to find many investigators inferring the presence or absence of alcoholism in Indian societies in light of preconceived notions about the nature of Indians themselves as well as about the causes and effects of alcoholism. (1974, 220–21)

This sums up the tribulations of alcohol-related research among American Indian tribes. Moreover, its impact upon governmental agencies in policy-setting decisions has great repercussions for Indian tribal and urban groups, for most of the research on American Indian and Alaska Native alcohol use is funded by federal agencies (Medicine 1983).

Sobriety Studies and Speculations

An early investigation by Field (1962) deals with sobriety. Essentially, his work is a critique of Horton's research on anxiety, and Field concludes that "drunkenness in primitive societies is determined less by the level of fear in a society than by the absence of corporate kin groups with stability, permanence, formal structure, and well-defined functions" (58). But, more appropriately, he bases his initial hypothesis of sobriety upon a "solidarity and respect" framework. He speculates that individuals in closely knit societies that operate on respect for authority tend to drink moderately and act passively when drunk. The Pueblo societies of native North America come to mind as contrastive to the loosely structured societies of the northern Plains. This interpretation, though seductive and seemingly applicable to American Indians of hunting and gathering groups, is but another study of correlates between social structure and drunkenness. Field's interpretations are based on coded materials in an analysis of early cross-cultural studies (Field 1962; McClelland et. al. 1972; Whiting and Child 1953), which were based on the Human Relations Area Files. There is no denial that societies with loosely structured, less well-defined social organizational features, with authority manifested in a diffuse manner, may be more prone to drunkenness. The Lakota data support this view, as control measures by kinship units were noticeably lacking (Goldfrank 1943; Mac-

Gregor 1945; Mirsky 1937; among others). However, the Lakota do not think of drinking as a problem and, more significantly, indicate that control is not part of the kin group's role.

In contrast, Levy and Kunitz found that the Hopi evidence a high incidence of cirrhosis of the liver. This tendency of the Hopi is fast becoming part of the folk wisdom regarding Indian alcoholism. Therefore, the following excerpt from Levy and Kunitz (1974) is important:

> Public drinking in the villages is virtually unknown among the Hopis. . . . When we examine the mortality rates from alcoholic cirrhosis, however, a different picture emerges (8). For the Navajos, the death rate from cirrhosis, even when age adjusted for people 20 years old and over, is slightly smaller than the national rate. For the general population, the age-adjusted rate was 19.9 in 1964. For the Navajos, it was approximately 15 during the period 1965–1967. The White Mountain Apaches' age-adjusted rate for the same three-year period was 44 per 100,000 annually. Surprisingly, the Hopi age-adjusted rate came to 104, which exceeded that of San Francisco, the highest reporting area in the nation. Although there are questions concerning the statistical interpretations of these differences that stem from the short periods we were forced to use for these tribes and from the very small populations of the Hopi and Apache tribes, we have concluded, for the present at least, that the Hopi rates are really higher than those for the other tribes. (100)

This is one of the few references to differential rates of cirrhosis deaths in the literature on Indian drinking. Certainly, no comparative data for tribes in the northern Plains is available. As indicated earlier, I was not allowed access to cirrhosis death information on Standing Rock reservation. Again, most deaths among them are often attributed to cirrhosis by the lay people on the reservation.

In his restudy of Standing Rock, Whittaker provides no information on the incidence of cirrhosis deaths. Instead, he relied upon Frederick's (1973) Indian Health Service statistics for all tribes: "Based on statistics compiled by the Indian Health Service, the death rate from alcoholic cirrhosis was 27.3 per 100,000 among Indians and 6.1 per 100,000 in all races. Alcoholic cirrhosis, in other words, is almost five times as high among the American Indians studied than among the non-Indian population" (Whittaker 1982, 31). This general data on cirrhosis does not seem to apply to the Lakota. Lakota imbibers tend to drink sporadically and enthusiastically, without any strictures from the kin group, or larger group, for that matter. It is still not clear, but one can surmise that the binge- or spree-drinking episodes of the Lakota do not seem to result in a high rate of cirrhosis of the liver. The fact that drinking periods are tied to availability of funds mitigates a persistent pattern of imbibing. The economic limitation has also been noted by other researchers (Leland 1976; Waddell and Everett 1980). Factors of contemporary dietary differences have not been investigated for any tribal group. One can indicate, however, that the first action Lakota persons (especially women) take when a kinsperson is, as they say, "coming off a drunk," is to feed the drunkard a meal. The meal contains beef, if at all possible. Again, a cultural orientation of meat as curative is evident. None of the studies regarding Indian alcohol use mentions dietary habits in conjunction with drinking behavior.

Despite the common and unquestioned bit of folk wisdom that "all Indians are drunks," there have been many persons—male and female—of Lakota ancestry who have not been drinkers. Complete teetotalers are declining in number. They generally range in age from thirty-five to eighty years. The Lakota women are the largest group in this segment. Some women in their seventies have never tasted liquor, except sacramental wines. These persons would fit in the category of total abstainers. There are some women who drank in their youth but who, upon reaching ages thirty-five to forty, stopped entirely and voluntarily. There is also one fifty-five-year-old woman, of the ten in her age cohort, who was a heavy drinker and stopped drinking. She became a Mormon. Of the ten persons in one community of ninety adults who were converted to Mormonism and became abstainers, following the nonalcoholic code of their new faith, four persons (including one married couple) began drinking two years after achieving sobriety. They explain their lapses as becoming "Jack Mormons."

By what means do the persons who, in reservation parlance, are the confirmed drunks, habitual drunkards, alcoholics, or *ito mani K'tca*—the supreme or ultimate drunks—achieve a continuous sober state? The major thrust of this research is directed toward the understanding of a new domain for the Lakota Sioux—that is, the achievement and maintenance of sobriety.

Pursuing the Sobriety Cause

Since the 1970s, governmental agencies, tribal governments, and Indian associations, such as the National Congress of American Indians, have exercised concern for the "problems" of alcohol use. Major interest converges upon intervention strategies, however unsuccessful many have been.

The dimensions of states of abstinence and sobriety in contemporary native societies have not generally been noted. In describing drinking styles among the urban Papago, Waddell and Everett (1980) indicate a rare glimpse of control:

> In a few instances, the supportive family relationships seem to have won out over the drinking group but the process has not been easy for the men who have this choice. In fact, it is difficult to predict how long the stabilized relationship will last. Some men report extended periods of sobriety and faithful performance of occupational tasks only to find themselves once again engulfed in the obligations of the drinking group. During the intermittent periods of occasional sobriety, there is good evidence that women were playing a strong, relatively stabilizing influence in their husbands' lives, even if their relationships were fraught with antagonisms. (69)

However, patterns of abstinence have been historically evident. This fact is outweighed by attributions of anomie or blurred by noting only the disadvantaged positions in the social structure of a superimposed society. Concerned native peoples seem to have ascribed to the "problem" orientation and have not looked to nonindulgence. As seen from the Lakota Sioux data, native beliefs of expected behavior based upon gender considerations, that is, male superiority and female subservience, are powerful forces at play in contemporary indigenous social systems as far as sobriety is concerned. Men drink because they are men.

Sobriety as an achievement seems based upon an enhanced awareness of self and society and certain introspective processes. Factors of age, sex, status, and economic state are important considerations. However, the social climate is also significant. Social movements and positive nativistic orientations may create a means to control drinking and assert abstinence patterns. After generations of cultural suppression and forced acculturation to the dominant society, it is only since the 1960s that a conscious revitalization movement has assumed ascendancy in most Sioux reservations and urban Indian enclaves. Allied to this resurgence is a new belief that alcohol is an introduced evil that was part of the genocide and ethnocide policies of the conquerors. This is a subtle orientation, verbalized in other contexts such as the American Indian Movement and other protest organizations. The ideologies of these new movements are important in current Indian life. Voluntary organizations such as the National Congress of American Indians and the North American Indian Women's Association have also delineated the problem of alcoholism among their constituencies. They often manifest their concern by giving workshops on the problem. Of importance is an increasing native awareness of the alcohol problem in Indian communities. Theories of control and abstinence within the context of Indian life are not generally evident. Externally imposed treatment methods, such as Alcoholics Anonymous and Antabuse use, have not proved successful among the Lakota or, for that matter, any other Indian group (Cooley 1980; Heath 1981). The dynamics of sobriety achievement explicated in any cultural matrix is needed. The area is clouded with a general search for a single causal explanation for Indian drinking. The milieu involved in voluntarily stopping the use and abuse of alcohol should be clarified.

The Lakota hold to the viewpoint that abstinence from imbibing in alcoholic beverages and sobriety are two different aspects in the total field of alcoholic intake. Abstinence is seen as never drinking, as in the Siouan *yat k'a shni*. Thus the Lakota notion of abstinence indicates that a person has never indulged in alcoholic beverages and maintains this stance. When Lakota people regard individuals who have previously been drinkers of intoxicants, they state, "wanna yat k'e shni," "that person does not drink." Lakota drinkers will often ask someone they might be considering as a potential recipient of alcohol, "ni yat k'an he?" or "Do you drink (alcohol)?" On the other hand, sobriety is envisioned as a stage a person elects to reach by self-determined action and a very conscious plan. This state is known as "dry" (*puza*), which metaphorically means "does not take in any liquid"— the liquid refers to alcoholic beverages. The path through which this sober state is reached is through the exercise of *chin k'a cha*, which best translates as "personal autonomy" or decision making and is often heard in reservation English as "willpower."

Sobriety as a Behavior

Drinking alcohol, simply called "drinking" or *yat k'an*, abstinence, and sobriety are regarded by the Lakota as distinct classes of behavior. The first category is mainly to drink in a social manner initially, but with the possibility for the drinking to turn into a prolonged bout or binge. This involvement depends upon the *chin k'a cha* configuration of the individuals who might be involved. Abstinence is not drinking at all, and Lakota abstainers are seldom participants in the group drinking events. They may be in a group—but abstain. In some drinking groups, the pressure to imbibe may become intolerable. Statements such as "You think you're too good to drink with us," or "I didn't know you're a *washichu* (white person)," or "So you're not a Lakota anymore" are examples of pressures to drink that can be unnerving to nondrinkers. In some groups who are drinking, if one states that one does not drink, one is seldom pressured to imbibe. This is not a usual pattern, however. Sobriety is a self-selected state that one achieves after being a "drinker." The common English term used on the reservation to denote this state is sober. The Lakota term *puza* is the native equivalent.

Sobriety as seen by Lakota persons is complete abstinence or nonindulgence in alcohol consumption. A continuing sober state may be examined on two levels. One concerns Lakota individuals who have never imbibed alcohol. Another level is a more important variable; it is composed of males and females who previously indulged in excessive alcohol use resulting in abuse but have chosen to quit drinking. The dynamics involved in this decision-making process is the critical issue needing explanation. Factors that have prompted this decision not to drink are the heart of this investigation. This continuing and stable sober state goes beyond the intermittent nondrinking that may be tied to lack of finances or opportunity to imbibe. Periodic abstinence is characteristic of much Indian drinking (Everett 1980; Hamer 1969; Lang 1979; Lemert 1958).

At this point, Jorgenson's (1972) model of "agentive" behavior has some pertinence. His insight of self-direction suggests that a person may assume a critical assessment of a social system and his role in it. It can therefore be postulated that an individual's resulting actions may have a significant behavioral change for the better. I suggest that the person will be leaving a state of dysfunction by enacting a personal action system that does not include intoxicants. The outstanding concern is for a careful analysis of the process of remolding one's life to cut down on and then stop drinking.

For this analysis, sobriety is defined as the achievement and maintenance of a continual sober state after a long period, perhaps years, of drinking excessively. That is, a sober state is deliberately sought and achieved. Excessive drinking would fit the Lakota definition of a drinker, or *ito mani s'a*, or one who drinks at the first opportunity—in other words, one who might be called a compulsive drinker. In reservation parlance, in the 1980s there was little distinction between the native definition of drinker and alcoholic, owing to the response to new prevention programs implemented by alcoholic workers. Despite these newer programs, as was noted by Whittaker in 1962, there appears to be a lack of knowledge by the majority of Lakota about the stages of alcoholism and the various symptoms and their manifestations. This raises issues of the efficacy of current educational programs on alcoholism.

There is, however, a general awareness of the increase in the use of alcohol on the reservation. Elders (sixty years old and older) expressed concern at such open forums as community meetings and in the more informal atmosphere of the ceremonial powwows, when speech making is common. Parents not only expressed a need for information regarding birth control for their teenage daughters but also tied teenage pregnancies to use of liquor. There was not, however, a demand for information on alcohol use (Gaalswyck 1979). In comparative terms of a decade ago, there is a growing acknowledgment of social problems, illegitimacy, consensual marriages, spouse and child abuse, and parental neglect, which are felt by the Lakota people to be based upon an abuse of alcohol.

The Lakota people are also cognizant of the fact that some of the tribal members have stopped drinking. This is an appreciated phenomenon, but it is not widely acclaimed—as is, for example, being a "good Lakota" traditionalist, being generous in giving feasts, or being a good powwow dancer. It appears that being "reformed"—as some Lakota say—has been part of the maturation process that some men have followed. However, it has not been a predictable event. White (1970) mentions "reformed" friends of the male clique in Rapid City but does not define them. Among the Standing Rock Sioux, "reformed" usually means that one has stopped drinking. The prevalent folk view is that being sober means not drunk. Being "reformed" is the complete nonuse of intoxicants. The cured state is seen as a permanent state reached by persons who heretofore had been heavy drinkers. Their description is "staying sober," or *yak k'e shni*, or "does not drink."

The sober state is unlike the state of abstinence that has been noted for some of the Lakota drinkers as a period between times of imbibing liquor. Leland (1976) reports a "total abstinence" and relegates the category to the "insufficient evidence" list. She uses the items enumerated by Jellinek (1952) and summarizes the ratings of Jellinek's symptoms of alcohol addiction among Indian groups.

Jellinek indicates that alcohol addicts often use periods of total abstinence to control drinking. Leland (1976) confirms this. Jellinek points out, however, that this decision seemed to be "in compliance with social pressures" (681). The specific contextual frame of the social system is of significance here, as Jellinek's formulations were mainly for American society. Data from the Lakota inebriates, plus other Indian groups (Hamer 1969; Horton 1943; Kunitz, Levy, and Everett 1969; Lemert 1958; Waddell and Everett 1980), indicate that periodic drinking is the predominant native pattern of alcohol use with periods of total abstinence occurring for a variety of reasons: lack of money, isolation from an alcohol source, periods of mourning, and incarceration. Lakota accounts reveal that periods of sobriety are neither self-imposed, generally, nor the results of conscious efforts to control drinking. It is apparent that abstinence from drinking is not a reaction to pressures to change based upon group censure. As indicated, social pressures of coercion are not strongly developed among the Lakota for maintaining sobriety.

The main reason for sobriety among confirmed drinkers is lack of cash or materials to exchange for alcohol. Whittaker's (1962) study reveals that 21 percent of the 208 respondents on Standing Rock indicated they drank primarily on weekends. At that time, there was no mention of persons who remained sober by choice. Since initiating the Whittaker study in 1961, the Standing Rock Commission on Alcoholism has not remained in force. There are similar organizations on this and other Lakota reservations. More prevention programs have begun with funds obtained from several governmental agencies; however, tribal programs for alcohol control have not been evaluated. Stephens and Agar (1979) recently assessed four anonymous programs—two in urban centers and two tribal programs. Their assessment indicated that, in general, the programs were badly administered and capricious in their treatments. In 1978, the National Institute on Alcohol Abuse and Alcoholism transferred mature programs (tribal programs that had been in operation for three or four years) to the U.S. Public Health Service. Leland (1977) viewed this as detrimental to established, unique, tribally specific programs. In general, evaluation has been partitive and premature, and results are seldom utilized in changing the nature of treatment programs.

Many of these programs, particularly the one at Standing Rock, espouse and encourage total abstinence. The Alcoholics Anonymous (AA) model has been the most widely implemented in most of the tribal programs. The model has not been noticeably successful on Standing Rock. For example, it seems difficult for Lakota individuals to stand up and recount autobiographical accounts of drunken behaviors and misdeeds as called for in the AA model. The patterns of recounting honorific achievements are the most accepted public accounting. Because of the nature of Sioux society, tight regulatory controls by persons in the in-group or kin group are not forthcoming. The lack of an effective communication system, that is, telephones, also accounts for the AA model's lack of success. Even though the new housing programs on the reservation have formed clusters of homes in contrast to the dispersed settlement pattern of the early period, direct personal intervention has not worked as a prevention measure.

Total abstinence is not typical behavior of many Sioux persons. Achieving that state is beset with many obstacles. The constant pressure to drink continues to be exerted by other Lakota persons. The major orientation of individuals to sharing and immediate gratification may override the consideration for control of drinking. Periodic "falling off the wagon" or, as the Sioux label it, a "slip," occurs. It usually coincides with the first of the month or the payment of leases within a kinship group, usually in December. For most persons, the resumption of drinking indicates that consciously sought abstinence periods are of a temporary nature. The periods are also difficult to distinguish from times when money is lacking.

Perceptions of Nondrinkers

Despite the folk saying of the Sioux that "everyone drinks," there are some individuals who, through a process seldom reported in the literature on alcohol use, have become and remained sober. Continued total abstinence as a new behavioral life-way has not been easily achieved by the persons who fit this category. Pressures to drink from the in-group were reported to be enormous. But there was also a bit of disbelief and taunting that occurred and was instigated by non-Lakota persons in the nearby border towns where much of the drinking was done. The first response to the sober person is one of disbelief by family and community members, as was also noted by Whittaker in the 1950s.

Given the almost complete involvement in alcohol consumption by the Lakota Sioux, especially males, on Standing Rock Reservation, my investigation focused upon the assumption of a sober state as a chosen act. From a Lakota perspective, drinking alcohol is not a deviant act. Few anthropological studies mention abstinence, so data for comparative purposes are sparse. Thus, it is novel to find a report such as the following:

> However, except for a number of women, there are few abstainers among the Naskapi. In fact I knew of only one adult male (sixty-five years old) who claims never to drink and whose claim is substantiated by others. Furthermore, he is a virtual recluse whose most frequent interactions are with some older Montagnais who, as far as I could gather, do not drink either. (Robbins 1973, 109)

There are two significant points in the above excerpt. One is that women tend to be abstainers; the other that the single man who does not drink is a recluse. This may be the only means by which he can maintain a sober state. Data on Indians who are sober, or achieve this state, is rare in the literature. Mention of sobriety as an item in the over eight hundred studies examined in 1980 yielded only the three studies by Lang (1979), Robbins (1973), and Waddell and Everett (1980).

In the entire decade of my observations in a border town situated between two reservations, there were only two women who might be classified by the police of this town as alcoholics. This classification is defined in Lakota terms as one whose dependence upon alcohol is complete—to the exclusion of all else. More specifically, these persons are estranged from family and kin group—except that when they have no place to go they return to "sober up," and they are accepted. These women spend their entire days cadging drinks from white men and visiting Indians alike. One of the females is sixty-eight years old and has lived this way for thirty years. The other was a relative newcomer to this lifestyle. She had been drinking since the 1970s and has made no attempt at rehabilitation. Native views were that "her mind is being affected by drink," and she is the object of pity and compassion by the group. This compassion is often expressed by giving money to these women who then convert it into liquor. To my knowledge, there were three women whose deaths were diagnosed as Laennec's cirrhosis in 1979 alone (personal communication from family members).

In examining generational differences among Indian drinkers a pattern emerges. Women tend to stop drinking when they reach the thirty-five-to forty-year-old category. This is explained simply by saying that they are *winyan tanka* ("women, big"), which has connotations of maturity in Lakota. When questioned further, they indicate that they are "too old to drink" or that "their children are grown, now." Some mothers said that when they attempted to reprimand their children about drinking, their past drinking days were used to negate their admonitions. Therefore, they felt that if they were to control their children, they should set an example. Maintenance of sobriety was not a difficult task for the majority of them. Many had become grandmothers and had assumed care of their grandchildren.

In contrast, the majority of Lakota males drink and do so excessively. Some of them also begin to level off in their drinking by the year forty onward. Some become complete nonimbibers. The most common response to the question, "Why did you quit drinking?" from the ten men who had achieved complete sobriety was, "I was tired of drinking and carousing." Many of them indicated that sobriety was not an easy road to follow. They specifically mentioned the taunts by the drinkers who urged them to drink with them; the lack of support groups, including kin; the loneliness encountered; and the lack of friends. Many of them indicated that the ridicule and disbelief in their new status was equally onerous from the white people in the towns. One informed me that when he went into the trading center, he was most often greeted with, "Well,

Chief! I remember when you used to drink!" He responded, "Yes, and I was a better drunk than you were!"

Folk Beliefs and Sobriety

Few folk beliefs exist about the onset of uncontrolled drinking among the Lakota today. A major deterrent used by the full bloods invokes the concept of *wacunza* or "to cause harm." Grobsmith (1974) interprets this concept as "imminent justice." In native views, an implicit and always unspoken consequence of this untoward act is to bring misfortune upon someone by one's action. Thus, if children cry needlessly or for no obvious reason, they are told that they are going to *wacunza* someone in their family. When one who has not been drinking (i.e., someone who has been in a sober state for some time) begins to imbibe alcohol, or if one who has never drunk liquor begins to drink excessively, the person is told that *wacunza* will result. This uncontrolled behavior is also thought to result in the injury of a closely related member of the *tiospaye*. A segment of the population also believes that excessive drinking after a death of a loved one can result in the habit of constant drinking. This is called *ah' yah,* "to make habit forming." Most traditional Lakota will not drink for a year, or at least six months, after the death of a closely related kin.

According to folk beliefs, women state that excessive drinking may cause miscarriages or stillbirths. The majority of women do not drink during pregnancy. For some, this may be a time when they give up drinking entirely. Ten young women in their twenties, who were carrying illegitimate children, often drank excessively but did not state a reason for this. This might be interpreted as a possible connection to causes of miscarriages. Answers to queries obtained from Indian Health Service personnel (native) gave no indication of Fetal Alcohol Syndrome (FAS). In 1980 the concern for this FAS is of an intertribal nature—and an urban phenomenon in a prevention mode. However, by the late 1980s, FAS was manifest in some Lakota reservations and concerns were evident.

Dimensions of Sobriety

Dimensions of sobriety and abstinence from intoxicants are not often mentioned in studies on Siouan drinking. Therefore, the much-lauded study by Whittaker (1961, 1962) is pertinent to the group under consideration. This study was commissioned by the Tribal Council on Standing Rock Reservation in the summer of 1961. His total sample was "208 subjects, equally divided between men and women representing the adult population"

(1961, 80). In his Iowan, white comparative group, religious beliefs or ethical considerations were often stated as reasons for nondrinking by many people. Some of the Standing Rock respondents offered health or efficiency as a reason for their staying sober. However, 40 percent of the Sioux sample could not offer an explanation for not drinking. In his report to the tribe, Whittaker (1961) notes that "47 percent of the Indian group either could not, or would not give a reason for abstaining. Discussion with Indian leaders concerning this and the large numbers of drinkers who did not give a reason for drinking revealed the general consensus that these people had very likely never given the matter much thought" (29). There is a slight discrepancy in the above internal report and the 1962 published one. The 1961 report gives a percentage of 47, but the number is 40 percent in the 1962 report. In the Sioux group, abstinence occurred in women when their children were born. Whittaker does not give numbers or ages of these women, nor how long abstinence obtained.

The Sioux group consisted of former heavy drinkers. Twenty-six percent of the Indian abstainers had previously indulged in drinking four or more times a week. In answer to the question Whittaker posed, "How can an alcoholic stop drinking?" 73 percent thought the drinker would require help and 6 percent thought religion would be the answer (Whittaker 1963, 83). The emphasis on willpower is striking. It is the closest English vernacular term for the Lakota concept of *chin k'a cha*, which might best be specified as self-actualization or exercise of personal autonomy in a decision-making process.

Whittaker emphasizes the lack of social control to mitigate excessive drinking. He states that the drinker was not punished. Any deviant or unusual behavior that happened while drinking was excused, and the drunk was incorporated immediately into the kin group. In reference to an earlier description of male superiority in Siouan society, he notes that women were expected to remain with a drinking spouse. Moreover, beating a wife when drunk was not disapproved of by 38 percent of the respondents to the question. These attitudes clearly suggest that deviant behavior is overlooked when the perpetrator is drunk. Whittaker (1963) finds that:

> Questioned about attitudes toward abstainers, 58 percent said they thought a person who refrains or refuses to take a drink is "commendable," 14 percent did not care one way or the other, 17 percent either did not know or expressed no opinion, 3 percent were hostile to such a person, 5 percent thought this must be a person of great will power, and 3 percent said they had never seen anyone refuse a drink and hence could not answer the question. (86)

When put in cultural context, several factors stand out. Not caring or knowing suggests noninterference, while hostility and reference to willpower are reflective of Sioux society. But apparently, the hostility feature is also found in another group. Describing the difficulties of Indian men maintaining sobriety in an urban setting in Minneapolis, Lang (1979) states:

> At the halfway house, there is a noticeable difference in response to a white counselor and an Indian counselor, though the Indian counselor runs into criticism by his fellows as acting "like a big man" just as "drinking buddies" who try to maintain sobriety and hold a job are maligned. This "leveling tendency" is perhaps as important as any external factor in the situational reality of trying to stop drinking. . . . Likewise, the rewards of stopping drinking are rarely realized—in other words, abstinence is not necessarily accompanied by employment in a good job, financial security, or stability in marriage or residence. Giving up alcohol means giving up a pattern of life that is much more complicated than simply abstaining from the beverage. (32)

Although the tribe, Chippewa, and the social setting are different, the deprecation and the leveling aspects are reminiscent of Lakota behaviors. MacGregor (1945) mentions the leveling aspects of Siouan society and points to the strong egalitarian ethic. This can also be seen in the "Oh, you're too good to drink with us" attitude of many Lakota drinkers. The lack of a system of rewards for sobriety appears not to have surfaced in either society.

Coping strategies for the nonutilization of alcohol are not easily delineated. Case studies of Lakota individuals clarify some of the underlying dynamics basic to individual motivation and adaptive means utilized in a move from dependence on alcohol to a state of maintained sobriety. One can discern that a continual state of soberness can eliminate the positive social interactions that drinking buddies provide for most Indian males. Isolation from the primary group of reference was seen as a desolate situation. Ridicule by the in-group and members of the dominant society were also difficulties for the sobriety seeker. Social isolation and ostracism are difficult choices for Lakota drinkers or, for that matter, anyone to accept.

Linguistic Difficulties in Translation

Eliciting material from persons to whom English is a second language poses several problems. Many persons who are called full bloods on the Lakota reservations speak the native language and often one must translate their responses into English. Thus the question, "Why did you quit drinking?" often yielded the response, "I just got tired of it." This is the translation of the Lakota utterance *Ta watl' yesni*, which has been translated as "totally discouraged" (Johnson and Johnson 1965) and has been interpreted in a psychological frame to be a manifestation of pathological behaviors. This term, when used as a rationale to stop drinking, is a convenient statement for an entire range of reasons. Their responses in the native language translate as "I was tired of not having a job," "I was losing my family," "My wife left me," "I felt I had no control over my life," or "My mother asked me to quit." Another person answered, "I quit after my daughter died and have not been drinking since." Some male respondents said, after a long pause, "I thought about the trouble the Sioux are in." This suggests an awareness on the part of the people that many of the dissonances of Lakota life—family deterioration; loss of Lakota values; spouse, child, and parental neglect; accident rates largely due to drunken driving; and petty crimes, especially stealing to obtain money to drink—are all related to abuse of alcohol. One man said, "Someone stole my commodities (surplus food distribution) and sold them to the 'green grocer'" (a white fence in the border town). This realization of addiction challenged him.

Many Lakota persons of either gender are aware that prolonged drinking is detrimental to their health and well-being or *t'a aya un* (positive mental health). Yet the responses as to what prompted them to stop drinking seldom mentioned the health factor. It is not uncommon to hear people verbalize a warning that "you're going to drink yourself to death," while they are drinking. Others are aware that they are "burned out at thirty." Generally, these cautionary statements, though indicative of dangers, do not serve as strong impediments to others.

Lakota Self-Analysis

It is imperative that a client's movement toward sobriety needs to be taken into account, no matter how weakly developed, in order to provide a realistic treatment program for Indian people. As some of the responses indicate, a period of introspection or an awareness of self seems to have occurred. A native phrase that is used to describe this phase is *ah wa bleza ki*, "to examine one's self"—to cogitate, to become introspective. This term involves a type of self-analysis in an indigenous frame. This phrase has great implications for a change in behavior and is based upon the psychotherapeutic beliefs of the Lakota people. When supplicants seek advice from a native practitioner *wapiya* (curer) or *wichasha wakan* (holy man) or *winyan wakan* (holy or sacred woman) and ask for aid—for either physical or mental disturbances—they are asked to *ah bleza* (examine) their behavior. The underlying premise is that unless one is able to think upon one's actions and place some perspective upon these acts, one is unable to deal with problems that are based on interpersonal relationships. If one is perturbed by the actions of another in a stressful situation, one might describe this to the practitioner, who very frequently states, "Tok'sha, he ahbleza ki" or, "Eventually, the person who is causing distress may examine his or her acts and will rectify the situation." This, admittedly, is a very diffuse modality. The process places the remedial behavior upon the self-awareness and reasonable character of the person who is causing the dissonance. This is the ultimate focus upon individual autonomy (*chin k'a cha*), which is so characteristic of the Lakota Sioux. There is no force outside the individual, such as *wakan* ("sacred, omnipotent power") or slight feelings of guilt, via the Christian ethic, that places the locus of control upon the individual. This, then, may offer an explanation as to why many Sioux relate an achievement of sobriety to willpower. The great emphasis on individualism, or at least individual decision making as to one's life chances and behavioral mode, is tied up in these concepts of personhood. This helps explain the lack of controls that reside outside the individual and why kinfolk elect to remain apart from the social control apparatus when it centers upon drinking and nondrinking behaviors.

The entire responsibility for decision making is placed upon the individual. The person is also allowed an unstructured freedom of choice by the equally significant term *chin k'a cha*, which also has connotations of "he or she prefers to be that way." When these terms are used, they signify that no force outside the individual is able to intervene and make any significant changes in the person's behavior. This is a delicate issue, for the Lakota person might at any time *wachinko* (most commonly translated as "to pout") and withdraw. This concept has been developed more explicitly elsewhere (Lewis 1975; Medicine 1983). The term denotes a conscious withdrawal from the social group (*tiospaye*). It also connotes aspects of individual self-assessment, meditation, and an individual coping strategy.

It appears, then, that intervention and behavior modification, which is the crux of sobriety, is self-induced and constructed in such a manner as to withstand the pervasive, calculated, and continuous pressure of a peer group—beginning with adolescents and continuing with age sets that are like the *kola*-ships (friendships or clique groups) that remain functional in contemporary Lakota life. These groups give meaning to Lakota males. The self-imposed withdrawal that characterizes sobriety is "tough," as many persons indicated.

A cross-generational and mixed-gender group of drinkers emerged after 1965, when the phenomenon was first observed. The single and most salient feature, counterproductive to achieving and maintaining sobriety, is the sustained pressure to drink, which begins at an early age for men. This also began to be true of Lakota females in the 1980s. The structures being built to counteract the push for drinking, the evolution of self-help systems and personal coping mechanisms to maintain a sober state, were in the 1980s in an incipient stage and extremely idiosyncratic, manifesting the establishment of individual autonomy.

Religious Renaissance and the Control of Alcohol
The Lakota Sun Dance

EALTH WORKERS HAVE BECOME increasingly aware that imposed treatment modes are often ineffective for Indian clients afflicted with alcohol problems. This conclusion led some federal agencies, such as the National Institute of Mental Health and the National Institute on Alcohol Abuse and Alcoholism, to fund programs that based treatment of alcohol abusers upon indigenous conceptions of control. Programs, such as the Medicine Men's Association on the Rosebud Reservation in South Dakota and the Mt. Baldy Rehabilitation Center near Los Angeles are but two examples of funded programs. The Sun Dance's importance to sobriety patterns and to a generalized cultural enhancement is the topic of this chapter. It presents data on the revitalization of indigenous religion, particularly the Sun Dance, which has been sought by some participants as a means of controlling excessive drinking. However, participation in the Sun Dance was not seen as a way to control drinking problems, and abstinence was not stressed by the religious practitioners.

The Sun Dance was suppressed among the Sioux people in the 1880s, and its reactivation has been a response to the needs of the individuals who, in many cases, feel that Christianity has not met individual Lakota needs. It was the major ceremony, symbolizing for the Lakota their relationship to the *Wakan Tanka* (Sacred Power). Within the Sun Dance ritual were many sacred rites: ear-piercing ceremonies for children, naming ceremonies, ghost-keeping feasts for deceased members, betrothals, and honoring feasts. The major feature of the ritual was sacrifice through self-determined mutilation of one's body. The belief was that offering the only thing one owned—one's body—was the ultimate gift for self and tribal welfare. Men had their pectoral muscles pierced and thongs tied to their muscles and the Sun Dance Pole. They danced to free themselves. Others had buffalo skulls attached to slits in their back torso muscles. Both men and women offered bits of flesh from their arms. All this was done to obtain personal advantage, but the totality of the religious experience was beneficial to the entire group. Men danced in fulfillment of a vow—if saved in battle; if a sick child recovered; if a vision was sought; if a shaman's role was desired. Virtuous maidens were chosen to select the Sacred Tree and a respected woman to represent the Sacred Pipe Woman.

The performance of the Sun Dance benefited the entire group, and they obtained sustenance and strength through attendance. The cultural mandates of the group—generosity, bravery, fortitude, and wisdom—were validated. Therefore, the prohibition of the Sun Dance meant the loss not only of rites and ceremonies but, more importantly, the loss of the sanctions of proper behavior and of social institutions. A weakening of tribal ethos followed the loss of supernatural sanctions. Proselytizing by various Christian churches ensued, and conversion to Christianity was seen as a survival mechanism. In sum, the entire substructure of a society and belief system was demolished.

Since 1955, when the Sun Dance was reactivated as a public event on the Pine Ridge Reservation, this religious ritual and others of a minor importance have proliferated in the contemporary life of Lakota Indians on most of the major Sioux reservations in South Dakota. The revitalization has instigated a moral code that prohibits the use of alcohol while involved in the ceremony. The Wounded Knee confrontation in 1973, the resultant harassment of Pine Ridge residents, and associated encounters with tribal, federal, and state police seems to have strengthened the Sun Dance encampment. At present, the intertribal and international character of the participants has centered upon Green Grass in the Cheyenne River Reservation in South Dakota, where the Sacred Calf Pipe of the *Ocheti Shakowin* (Seven Council Fires of the Lakota nation) has traditionally been lodged.

During the turbulent 1960s, increased activism and articulation of Indian needs and demands can best be seen in such protest groups as the American Indian Movement (AIM). A major symbolic act of being a traditional Native American was "to Sun Dance" and, eventually, "to pierce." Participation in this ritual became a symbol of traditionality and served as an ethnic marker to many native peoples of all tribes—those in the American Indian movement, those who lived in urban areas, and those whose quest for identity necessitated a search for a symbolic and ritual system. The Sun Dance, with its history of repression by the U.S. government, plus an expression of the torture element, seems to have met the needs of many contemporary Indians.

The significance of the participation in a traditional religion transcended tribal affiliation. Urban Indians of Lakota heritage (from Seattle, the Bay area in California, Denver, and Chicago) returned to dance. Anishinabe (Chippewa) Indians were encouraged to participate in this ritual, which belonged to their traditional enemies. Only one Anishinabe indicated that he knew it was a Lakota rite, and as an Anishinabe, he had no right or desire to participate. Micmac Indians from New Brunswick, Canada, felt obligated to regain an Indian identity by making a pilgrimage to Sioux reservations—even if they did not participate in the ceremony. Members of AIM used participation as a new badge of commitment. The intertribal character of the participants through time has not been tabulated. One can gauge the increase of dancers when one calculates the increase of fifty-seven dancers in the 1976 Sun Dance at Green Grass to ninety dancers in 1978. Since 1975, the Minneconjou Indian Culture Society from the Museum at Eagle Butte apparently has given substantial monetary aid—both in advertising with printed posters and with the supply of food and gas money for the dancers and the principal medicine men. Assessment of the impact of the latter two factors is not readily available at the present time. The director of the museum is a returned urbanite whose husband has been an actor in the Hollywood movie industry. The Sacred Pipe still remains in the family who has had it for generations. In 1977, the proscription that the Pipe Bundle not be opened mandates activities around it. The Pipe Bundle's Keeper's father is increasingly active in such rituals as naming ceremonies, funerary rites, and mourning ceremonies.

The Sun Dance and its ritualists—leaders and intercessors—have been treated descriptively in Mails (1978) and mentioned by Powers (1977). There is little theoretical implication to the study of a revamped belief system among contemporary American Indians in these books. The theoretical contributions of Wallace (1956) in revitalization and mazeway resynthesis models and Aberle's (1966) "cultural deprivation" formulations are important in the analysis of such revivalistic movements. A further refinement in understanding ritualists and their impact upon such contemporary religious movements needs investigation. For the present-day Lakota, the aspects of such revitalization movements are often of a "reformative" nature. The individual motivation and rationale for involvement in such a movement is often absent in the data on religious revivals. In developing a theory, Hopen's (1964) term "reformative" may have some relevance. His suggestion to include aspects of cultural and psychological processes, social organization, and cause or motivation of individuals seems reasonable. These formulations, though often included in most anthropological analyses, have special connotation for many of the individuals involved. Most native participants are often not aware of such things as social organization and the value orientations underlying these movements. They have their own motivations. In attempting to develop a topology of social movements, Kopytoff (1964) refers to "reformative" movements as a cluster of "'ideological referents,' and a desire to change existing culture or parts of it" (86). It appears, therefore, that a problem to be solved by the social movement is an important facet of the current resurgence of ritual behavior among some Lakota people. In this case, the problem to be solved, or at least minimized, is that of excessive alcoholism on many of the Sioux reservations. Other solutions are redress of economic and social deprivation and extreme poverty and a disadvantaged position in a dominant and racist society. In addition, participation in the Sun Dance is an important political statement for many and a means of establishing ethnic identity. To others, it is a more meaningful belief and action system.

Further, Aberle's (1966) term "redemptive" has significance—or the primary objective of current Sun Dance participation is to seek change for individuals. Other features further refined by Jorgenson (1972, 7) are the criticism of a social system and the focus upon the remolding of the individual. The process by which the individual is changed, as in his relationship to others, is an important consideration. The notion of current revitalization movements, such as handing power to the powerless, will be a useful tool to further enhance an understanding of the processes involved. It is plausible to develop a model of comprehension of what Jorgenson calls an "agentive" approach to social action to understand the dynamic ramifications of alcohol control in a ritual setting.

At the present time, explorations into Seligman's (1975) concept of "learned helplessness" and Becker's (1973) positive approaches for individual actualization have pertinence for individual motivational analysis. Learned helplessness as a phrase denotes many behavioral patterns of contemporary Lakota men. Becker's ideas suggest that indulgence in alcohol among Lakota people may have assumed an ideological context.

Examining the dynamics of motivation in individual Lakota for involvement in the Sun Dance, there is little that would give clues for a generalized native approach for participation. Individual decisions to participate are the norm. The participants gather for the ritual and disperse immediately after its performance. On account of gender-based proscriptions in space allocation, it is almost impossible for a female to interview male participants if one follows the rules, as sexes are segregated in the ritual.

After the 1976 Sun Dance, seven participants who were from Standing Rock Reservation indicated that their search was for a new and individual transformation. The change is calculated, and the individual's relationship to others is altered. For these Lakota males, the experience was to restructure a place in a universe inhabited by kinspersons and in which a new awareness gained in the ritual would have greater impact upon their future lives. To them, the words of the Sun Dance song had great motivating powers: "wani 'ktacha hecamuwe"—"I will live, thus, I do this." This phrase also has a larger metaphorical meaning: "That my people may live." The impact of participation is to achieve a more meaningful life, a richer life—and to some—a life free of intoxicants.

Though this is not the aim of Mails's (1978) book, the rich descriptive accounts of the ritual and symbolic forms and the difficulty in obtaining articulate reasons for each dancer are acknowledged. However, Mails's book is the first published account of why some Lakota people danced. The explanations are obtained through taped interviews with William Schweigman, the principal leader. The biography of Fools Crow (Mails 1979) did not offer more information on individual dancer motivation.

Complication in Understanding Traditional Ceremonies

A native interpretation and rationale for becoming interested in an indigenous revitalization movement is generally lacking in the literature. This is especially true for American Indians. Bharati (1974) raises an interesting point: "The question of whether an anthropologist's being born and raises in an informant or subject society affects his work is certainly an interesting one" (258). This would hold equally for those innovators who are in a sense attempting to reconstruct a belief system to meet changing times and specific needs. Further, he states, "The ultimate reduction in the study of religion seems to lie in symbology. I suggested earlier that we might be better off if we jettisoned symbol talk altogether in the investigations of religions that do not use 'symbol' emically" (262). Bharati emphasizes the need for a

> definitional genre, built on a linguistic matrix of a set of ethnosemantic data. A linguistic theory might generate the logical deduction of a belief pattern that might then be called a symbol. In an ethnosemantic theory, the actors themselves would create a body of stipulated meanings capable

of being conventionalized, from which "ex-post-fact" symbols could then be deduced. (262)

This could happen if the current group of Lakota medicine men and ritualists had met in such organizations as the Medicine Men and Associates at Sinte Gleska University and attempted to examine the structure of the new religious revival. The beginnings of this seemed apparent, for many of the apprentices who are articulate both in Lakota and English were attempting to deal with ethnosemantic and underlying philosophical rubrics. The beginnings of an actor-induced analysis could be utilized as an eliciting tool in the development of indigenous symbols. This model could also be followed in Lakota drinking and sobriety studies.

Presentations of Sun Dance Data

The publication of Mails's 1978 book on Sun Dances has been criticized by the Lakota studies personnel at Sinte Gleska. This is perhaps understood in view of the detailed account of the mismanaged traditional Sun Dance sponsored by the college, which is reported in the book. Their further disenchantment is that the Mails report relies primarily on Schweigman's (Chief Eagle Feather) performances and interpretations. Nonetheless, Mails's book does give comparative materials and adds much to our knowledge of current ritual. Furthermore, one intercessor, who was trained by Peter Catches and was assistant to Fools Crow, states that Mails's book is "too superficial" and does not deal with "the philosophical and theological viewpoints of the participants." At the present time, the complete individuality of the various Sun Dance leaders and intercessors has apparently been so concentrated upon ritual performance that the philosophical and symbolic aspects of the belief system have remained largely unexamined. This is equally apparent in the reasons for each pledger's performance. There are a few native intercessors who are examining their own motivations and actions as ritualists and are speaking about this religious experience. There are a number of variables that must be considered in this trend toward self-assessment. These include linguistic proficiency in both English and the native language, reservation versus urban residence, early socialization processes regarding religious affiliation, and rationale for return to native theology.

Propriety and Traditional Practices

Proper behavior and individual autonomy in Lakota, as well as Sun Dance behavior, is expressed in the following incident. Eagle Feather's

(Schweigman) grandson wished to be pierced when he was only nine years old. Schweigman's cohorts in his twenty-three years of Sun Dance participation all refused his request for someone to do this. One said: "I'm not pure enough to pierce the little man. I drink and I run around with women. I've done wrong and I am a sinner. I can't pierce the little gentleman because so far his life is so pure that I'm not worthy to touch him that way" (Mails 1978, 50). This utterance brings up certain factors that are important in assessing attitudes in several dimensions. Aspects of drinking and sexual relations are placed in the same category as sin in the Christian context. More pertinently, the lack of social controls over drinking in modern Sioux reservation lifestyle makes these statements of expected behavior more difficult to assess the measures of ritual life in sobriety maintenance. Mails (1978) points out parameters of the alcohol situation:

> It is evident that the majority of the modern-day vows find their impetus in the devastating liquor problem which plagues the Sioux reservations. Moving steadily like a grim reaper, it destroys lives and homes with a vengeance awesome to see. It is, in the view of every medicine man and leader, a curse of incredible proportions. To make matters worse, the influx of cheap drugs is compounding the situation daily. Other reasons for present-day vows are ill-health and poverty. On occasion, too, it serves political expediency to take in the dance. (43)

Table 7.1 has been reconstructed from the taped and transcribed interviews, which Schweigman apparently gave to Mails. The reasons for participation are distilled through Eagle Feather's observations. At this time, it is very difficult to ascertain whether these reasons were given to the Sun Dance leader (Schweigman) as a rationale or, in taping them, he attributed these reasons to the participants. Schweigman died in 1979.

The nondrinkers were Albert Stands, sixty-five years old, and George Elk, seventy-nine years old. The latter died in March 1978. One part of the Sun Dance at Rosebud is the opportunity given each pledger to come to the public address system and indicate the reasons for participation. Mails (1978) states that "on these occasions it is common to include a confession of past sins, such as excessive drinking or other bad behavior" (44). Public confession is not apparent at other Sun Dances, which reflects the wide variations in its performance, and they are not a part of the ritual at Standing Rock.

Of special significance in the curing aspects of alcohol addiction is the case of C.Q. We are told that he became "demon possessed," according to Eagle Feather (Mails 1978, 59), began drinking, and finally went to live

Table 7.1.   Reasons for Participating in the Sun Dance

Name	Reservation	Age	Reason for Dancing
L.H.	Father-Cheyenne Agency	16	To unite family splintered by alcoholism (mother in treatment center, siblings in foster homes)
Gilbert Yellow Hawk	Rosebud	42	Drinking (abstinent since 1973)
Jerry Dragg	Yankton	25	Drinking (abstinent since 1973)
C.Q.	Rosebud	43	Drinking (began drinking, saw psychiatrist, nonbeliever in both native and white belief systems now)
Kermit Bear Shield	Pine Ridge	?	To regain own health
Reuben Fire Thunder	Pine Ridge	?	For daughter to regain health
Orrie Farrel	Standing Rock	25	For health of mother, father, and sister (He drinks, but apparently, this was not part of his reason)
B.M. (female)	Rosebud	35	Health and financial help for father (implicitly, financial aid for self)
Robert Black Feather	Canadian	?	No reason attributed except believes deeply in Indian religion (Father is Sioux, Mother is Spanish)

Compiled (Mails 1978, 47–60)

with a brother in Minneapolis. Schweigman continues: "While he was in Minneapolis after this, a psychiatrist got hold of him. We had wanted to arrange something like that here, but there wasn't any available at the time. The worst part is that the psychiatrist said C.Q. had been a religious fanatic and was lost because of religion" (Mails 1978, 59–60).

It is extremely significant that although the search for sobriety has entered the realm of the Sun Dance, the code for social control has not solidified into rules of restriction, nor has it been obvious that a charismatic leader has arisen. It seems possible that the very individualistic character of Lakota people, which has been noted by many ethnographers (Erikson 1939; Hassrick 1961; MacGregor 1945), would negatively influence such a development. Another strong feature is the so-called "leveling process," which is sometimes attributed to Lakota culture. In 1980 there was insufficient data on individual personalities of the Sun Dance leaders and intercessors to make a final statement in regard to charismatic qualities.

As for the return to native beliefs, another viable ritual, the *yuwipi*, is not utilized, except as a confession feature in order to control excessive ingestion of alcohol and its related problems. There are other ritual acts, such as *wopila* (to give thanks) and *ochoka* (in the center), that are used for therapeutic measures but seemingly not to cure alcoholism. These last two rituals deal with stress and anxiety.

My main concern here has been the examination of the Sun Dance ritual as a means to maintain alcohol abstinence. It has not been entirely efficacious. Because the Sun Dance among the Lakota Sioux has had such a relatively recent revival, the latent functions are still to be assessed. There were twenty-five Sun Dances held in South Dakota in 1986. It seems to manifest the more positive aspects of being an American Indian or Lakota. One can postulate its reinforcement of cultural identity—not only for Sioux people but also for persons from other tribes who participate in it. The ethnic marker designation is certainly a dominant feature. Its function as a deterrent against total acculturation is one feature that can form the basis for future research. It is suggested that control of alcohol and other drugs will be an important mandate for participation. This is especially significant to combat increased drinking as indicated by Whittaker (1982). This corroborates my long-range observations of a general increase of alcohol consumption at an earlier age by both male and female Lakota.

Since the resurgence and emergence of many medicine men and ritualists is increasing, the future and direction this movement takes will also be reflected in the reformative aspects of alcohol use and control.

Siouan Sobriety Patterns

8

"I Was a Better Drunk Than You Were"

THE ABOVE QUOTE IS A RESPONSE of a Sioux male to a white businessman in a neighboring border town and indicates the unbelievable nature of sobriety when it is manifested among Lakota Sioux. The preceding materials suggest that tremendous social pressures generated by their own ethnic group plus the economic profits to be accrued by the purveyors of alcoholic beverages militates against abstinence among the Indian population.

This chapter will present the ephemeral nature of the majority of Lakota drinkers' attempts at maintaining sobriety. The concentration, however, is upon the character of more enduring and successful attempts to rid one's self of drinking *minnewakan* (magic water) and the coping strategies associated with sobriety.

Multicultural Nature of Indians

Frequently stated in this work is the fact that alcohol use and its sociocultural manifestations among Indian people have been pervasive. A generalized image that "Indians are all drunks" has emerged in the literature. The thesis to be argued here is that American Indian societies represent distinctive cultural units. Each enclave represents tribal-specific cultural forms. Although this fact is recognized by most responsible researchers (Ferguson 1966, 1968; Levy and Kunitz 1971a; Westermeyer 1974), a tribally specific report is often interpreted to cover the entire spectrum of extant tribes (Waldram 2004). This fact is especially pertinent to policy makers in state and federal governments. It is, however, a commonplace fault in social scientific research.

Westermeyer (1972) has pointed to the variation in drinking behavior intertribally, intratribally, and individually. Patterns of control of alcohol use have varied. Historically, there have been many persons—male and female—who have not touched alcohol. There is little hard data on persons in this category, as noted previously. Many women did not consume alcohol until after its purchase was made legal for Indians in 1953. Whittaker (1962) indicates a discernable increase in the number of women who drink on Standing Rock Reservation. On the other hand, most men have imbibed at some time in their lives. Most of them began drinking during adolescence. Some have diminished their use of liquor, others imbibe at specific times—holidays, rodeos, and powwows—and still others drink whenever and wherever liquor is available.

There is a wide range of individuals who drink in discernable patterns. Some drink at any time and would be labeled as heavy users of liquor by any standard—white or Indian. These heavy drinkers were self-selected in the sense that these persons were the only ones who attempted to achieve sobriety after a long period of intensive utilization of alcohol. None of them, according to their reports, was warned by any medical practitioner that one had to quit drinking. No attempt was made to utilize the medical records of these persons. The writer is a member of the tribal group and maintains a home on the reservation. Furthermore, strong ethical considerations were reasons why this avenue was not pursued. Private records are often used indiscriminately, and therefore, many Indians are becoming disenchanted with social scientists (Maynard 1974). Research with a new orientation on alcohol use among Indians institutionalized in halfway houses or in treatment programs became popular in the 1970s. They form a group of Sioux for captive research (Uecker, Boutilier, and Richardson 1980). This particular report, relying upon the Minnesota Multiphasic Personality Inventory (MMPI), indicated the psychopathology that forty Sioux males revealed was "primarily neuroticism and related to identification with Indian heritage" (661). The Richardson Indian Culturalization Test (ICT) is a twenty-five-item multiple-choice test developed to examine "Indianism" by allowing the respondent to choose such items as problem drinking, drunken violence, deprivation, and work only when in need of money as an indication of a high degree of Indian culture. The ICT is a very ambiguous instrument that has not undergone an item analysis. The salient point of Uecker, Boutilier, and Richardson is that many of the Indian men, mainly Sioux, were severely malnourished. Certainly this fact would have some relevance to such alcohol diagnosis statements as "acute brain syndrome." Another significant feature of the ICT is the use of the Lakota

language as a social indicator of "traditional Indian ways." It is such inade-
quately validated research that has posed an unclear picture of alcohol use
among Indian people.

After generations of adaptation to a dominant, superimposed society,
each tribal group has made distinctive adjustments. There is a decided variation in alcohol use from one tribal enclave to another. I have previously
cited such outstanding and sustained researchers as Levy and Kunitz
(1971a) who have indicated variance in alcohol use among such tribes as
the White Mountain Apache, the Hopi, and Navajo. Everett (1980) designates two common themes regarding Indian drinking. He feels that "'Indian Drinking' is somehow different than non-Indian drinking" (xiv).
Moreover, he indicates that all its abuses aside, a number of positive aspects
are embedded in alcohol use among Indian groups. A more recent study,
concentrating on native peoples in the North, indicate that Hamer and
Steinberg (1980) hold to this view:

> It has long been recognized that patterns of alcohol consumption differ
> greatly between Native North Americans and the people of European an-
> cestry who brought this trait to the New World. Although a number of re-
> cent studies show that the volume of alcohol consumed by Native people
> is not proportionately greater than that consumed by other groups, the so-
> cial cost does appear to be proportionately high. Native populations suffer
> an enormously high arrest rate for alcohol-related offenses, and there are
> pervasive evidences of alcohol-based disruption of ordinary life patterns.
> These facts point to significant variation in drinking styles. (1)

Based upon my long-term observation of the drinking patterns on Standing Rock Reservation, they initially comprised quick consumption and
surreptitious methods owing to the legal restriction on alcohol use that
ended in 1953. This is called "chug-a-lugging" in reservation vernacular,
and *enaxtche-yat ka* in Siouan, which translates as "drinking quickly." Soli-
tary drinking is absent owing to the effects of peer groups and the sharing
syndrome. Spree or binge drinking predominates as a pattern with consumption of liquor until monetary and liquid resources are exhausted. Then
"passing out" or comatoseness ensues. A pattern of drinking is established
early in the socialization process of children observing and imitating adult
behavior regarding drinking alcohol. There is slight, or no, disapproval by
the kin group or the community. The drinker's family serves as a protective
buffer for the drinker and offers little censure or control. From 1953 to
1973, drinking increased among both males and females on Standing Rock
Reservation. By 1980 a drinking style of consumption in the home

emerged at celebrations, such as birthdays, holidays, and special events. This may be a class differentiation that reflects other social factors such as involvement in higher education, work in federal and tribal agencies, and a greater involvement in the dominant society. Extensive interaction off the reservation in turn fosters greater use of alcohol among some Lakota people. There is still the ubiquitous "Indian bar" in most border towns that attracts transient and resident Indians alike. However, a pattern of drinking cocktails before dinner or wine with dinner is observable. Drinking beer at cookouts is becoming more common, as are alcohol consumption patterns at some social events, such as powwows. Many of these latter events post signs that read "No liquor or *pezi* (grass) allowed." This sentence signals the intrusion of other drugs. The ingestion of drugs, however, is surreptitious.

Whittaker's 1982 restudy of Standing Rock states that alcohol use has increased since his 1950s investigation and has stabilized at a high rate. He also notes that overtly, there are more alcohol-related physical manifestations that may be responsible for more individuals seeking sobriety. In my investigation, I found a more voluntary disengagement from excessive drinking and a more calculated return to a native belief system that may offer a more satisfactory coping mechanism.

In summary, these postulates guided my analysis for Lakota Sioux cultural data.

1. Ethnohistorical precedents are important considerations in the current manifestations of Indian drinking. As a learned activity, patterns of consumption and attitudes that direct this utilization vary and are tied to the indigenous milieu and the methods of introduction of the substance.
2. Pathological traits are a part of alcohol use in any society. Definitions of pathologies are contextually defined. Certain qualitative differences are amplified in behavioral configurations for several reasons. Behavioral elements such as aggression, risk taking, and suicides are delimited by each group. Alcohol use, moreover, may be a creative adjustment to conditions of deprivation—social and economic—contingent upon entry into a new social system.
3. Indigenously inspired change to control excessive and debilitating use of alcohol may be involved in social movements for revitalization of repressed cultures. Invigorating an entire society seems necessary for such reformist movements to be effective. Moving from an ethic based upon persuasion, it must eventually become standard setting to achieve its aims.

4. As with many subcultural patterns within an encompassing society, tribal groups have perpetuated a drinking style that is a product of ethnohistorical and unique cultural interpretations. For the Lakota Sioux, change would appear to be contingent upon reorientation in socialization patterns, changes in social structural configurations, and increases in resources that are earned with equity and dignity. Resources may be social or economic.

Trimble and Medicine (1976) constructed a model that was multicelled and included factors seen to be important for delineating features of mental health categories. The drinking of alcohol, which results in behaviors often labeled as deviant, seems an integral part of the mental health of Indians. Our model attempted to obviate fragmented and partial conclusions regarding drinking behavior. It is suggested that such a formulation might adequately cover the multifaceted nature of alcohol use. This suggestion would allow a combination of ethnological, psychological, physiological, ecological (environmental), economic, and political variables to be included. The model also allowed some freedom in the combination of these items. It would also foster the combination of several methods and approaches. As indicated, studies on Indian alcohol use have tended to be based upon few explanatory features—anomie, dependency, powerlessness, social disintegration, or other pathological parameters.

The proposed schema was set out as all-inclusive and was predicated upon interdisciplinary teams working in contemporary Indian communities. For purposes of this examination, the sociocultural and psychological components have been emphasized. These are the postulates that guided the research:

1. When alcoholism reaches epidemic proportions and the structure of the society is threatened, some persons may develop strategies that allow these individuals to achieve and maintain sobriety (Aberle 1966; Jorgenson 1972; Wallace 1956, 1959, 1969). On the macrolevel of tribal concern, redemptive revivals (Sun Dance, Hocoxa—"throwing a voice," and Vision Questing) of the traditional society are being restored to deal with societal dissonance and individual maladjustment (alcoholism and associated dysfunctions).
2. On an individual level, tribal members are developing coping strategies to transcend alcohol addiction and selecting alternative lifestyles and a "conscious collective affirmative" (Becker 1973) in

which individuals may reaffirm self-worth. A return to a traditional belief system or a reassessed worldview and participation in new sodalities that serve as a satisfying support system is developed and utilized.

3. On an individual level (no charismatic leader has yet emerged), "learned helplessness" (Seligman 1975) and concomitant reactions to administered human relationships and self-deprecation are transferred to a greater self-awareness and self-actualization. The strategies for survival are redirected to a life without dependence upon alcohol.

4. Newly superimposed belief systems have replaced others as a means of dealing with alcohol abuse. Joining a new religion, that is, Mormonism, which puts strong prohibitions upon alcohol consumption, has formed a new support system for some tribal members of other and more traditional Christian faiths, and offers a more realistic way of dealing with a problem of alcoholism.

These and other suggested hypotheses have formed the analysis of the dynamics of alcohol abstinence among contemporary Lakota Indians.

Native Drinking Categorical Types

There are still, however, native definitions that have directed the sobriety seekers' cognitive frames. Motivational patterns may be expected to vary correspondingly with community expectations. Folk definitions are important indicators of drinking styles. Thus, these articulations are action oriented:

1. "Drinks like an Indian" as opposed to "drinks like a white" presents an operational rubric in contemporary Lakota life.

2. "Drinking like an Indian" means drinking to excess or stupor, or until the end of the bottle or monetary resources.

3. "Drinking like a white" means imbibing at restaurants and drinking only on weekends or the end of a work activity. There are no such social events as cocktail parties, brunches, or wine and cheese events in the lifestyle of the reservation folk. This category of persons might also be designated gatekeepers for they often are in positions to give jobs to the less well educated.

These native categories would fit persons into the classification of lower class or the "culture of excitement" (White 1970), with those Indians who fit into category 2 exhibiting the lack of awareness of a time orientation, with immediate gratification plus a lack of thrift as a way of life. This is the frame into which most of the case histories fall.

At the present time some Lakota Sioux individuals are emerging as participants in the last category of natives. These persons are members of the steadily employed. They work for federal agencies, tribal government, and educational agencies on the reservation. They drink at conferences and occasionally slip into binges with some of the hardcore drunks in the second designation. Those persons who might be labeled the "native elite" are the most defensive about their drinking habits.

The following are composite profiles. After collecting case studies from twenty Lakota males, I sorted them into categories—as to type of school attended, time of exposure to alcohol that propelled the person into drinking, family situation, and other characteristics. I then presented a composite of a "person." This was to obviate a further stereotyping by having some readers use individual cases as proving the image of the Indian drunk. This might also temper the interpretation and place the profiles within the cultural context in a patterned manner, rather than as an idiosyncratic isolate. Of greater consequence was the ethical consideration. Positive identification of a specific individual would be more difficult to pinpoint.

Case A

A youngest son in a family of eight, this forty-year-old Lakota Sioux male began drinking when he was ten years old. He stole liquor from his older brother who had returned from the Korean War. Throughout his youth, he drank surreptitiously when he was in a parochial boarding school on a Sioux reservation. He left the reservation during the relocation period of the 1950s and began a migratory trail of urban nomadism, beginning at seventeen years old when he dropped out of school upon his mother's death.

He "did terrible things when he was drunk," such as panhandling, "rolling people for money," and sleeping on sidewalks, besides spending much time in jails for being drunk and disorderly. One day, after an illness in a hospital, he decided that he was "tired of it," and decided to become sober. He prayed, and felt that if there was a God, he might be helped. He said, "I don't want to go to hell; I've been there." He pushed the bottle away at the next drinking encounter, and hasn't touched the bottle since. He has not consumed alcohol for five years.

The most difficult part in maintaining sobriety was the pressure exerted by former drinking buddies who often taunted him with accusations of "being too good to drink with them." He felt that an important means of coping with social ostracism from his former drinking group was voluntary isolation and "being busy." This person realized that his life would be wasted, so he decided to change his drinking pattern. He stated that he "thinks about things a lot," and keeps busy by going on long walks. He feels that his willpower and keeping busy maintain his sober state. He now works as a counselor in an alcoholism program. He is a full blood and lives with his girlfriend, a twenty-year-old white woman. He stated that the hardest part of this adjustment was that people stared at them when they went out.

Case B

He is a thirty-five-year-old Lakota Sioux male who moved to an urban area in 1975, after living in a large city near his reservation. His reason for assuming sobriety was that he felt he "was wasting his life by drinking." He has maintained a sober state for two years, after drinking since he was seventeen years old. His immediate concern is not to be involved with any Indians. This means that he consciously avoids any contact with them except at work, which is an alcohol treatment center. He never goes to powwows in the area, for he feels that the pressures to drink are too great and that he may not be able to resist them. Although he works in the field of alcohol control, he is weary of the accolades he receives because he has given up drinking. He feels that "they were not quite deserved." This prominence appears as part of his job as an alcoholism counselor. It fits the common perception in Indian alcohol control that one has to be a reformed drunkard in order to work effectively with alcoholics. He, too, "did bad things" when he was drinking. His prime reason for quitting was that he felt he "had to think about his life and plan for the future." Therefore, he stopped drinking alcohol.

Case C

This man is a forty-three-year-old Sioux, a reservation resident who quit drinking five years ago (1974). For him, it was a gradual tapering off. He began thinking about his drinking problem when his mother asked him why he drank so much. "Are you getting rich from drinking? Do you see a future in it?" she asked. These utterances are his translations from her conversation in Lakota. "Try and quit," she said. "I might be leaving this world and there will be no one to look after you."

During this time, he was blacking out and "running people off the road," and was not aware of this behavior. It was only when people told him that he had "run them off the road" that he was aware of the extent of his drinking problem. He began thinking about his drinking pattern, and said, "It was kind of hard."

He began saying, "No" to his friends when they asked him to drink. He began losing his friends. At this time, he set limits to his drinking. For two years he observed other people. He saw a "sober side of life." That is, he saw that those persons who did not drink held jobs. He decided to "help his folks and bought them a home." He was beginning "to gradually face reality."

During this time, his friends were waiting for him "to fall again," that is, to begin drinking. During this time, he used Antabuse for two weeks. He drank a can and a half of beer. He began his third can of beer. His heart started to beat quickly, and his eyes started to turn red. He was frightened. He said that during the two-year period beginning his sober state, the "hardest thing for me to do was to go to someone's house and refuse a drink." He felt that white people think that all Indians drink. This makes it "more difficult for him." There was ridicule from the white persons he interacted with as they did not believe that he had quit drinking.

Why did he want to quit drinking? He made a vow to himself, and he thinks the decision was tied in with his mother's statements. He is now becoming involved in traditional Indian religion. He has helped set up the sweat lodge (*Ini pi*). The "use of Indian medicine has also helped." By this he means that medicine men have prayed for him, and this has been supportive. Essentially, their prayers have shown him that somebody cares and assists him in keeping his vow. He feels reassured that someone believes he is sincere about his plan to quit drinking. He feels that other persons (i.e., Catholics) who prayed for him "were praying from the lips and not from the heart."

Now he feels somewhat more secure. If his friends tease him about drinking, he does not "pay any attention to them." The woman with whom he is allied in a consensual union buys liquor. He does not bother with it. He did try Alcoholics Anonymous, but it was of no avail. He does not believe that the program "helps the Lakota people." He thinks that "people cannot tell other people what to do." His first wife was a Lakota Sioux. They had four children.

He began drinking when he was in the army where he "drank a lot." He was in the army for three years with an overseas experience. He became interested in other things during this time in the service. Initially, he was shy and "kept to himself," but by living with other people he overcame his shyness. His first service experience was in the South. He was somewhat bothered by segregation but got along well with both blacks and whites in the service.

He now has a job in the community and also serves on the school board. He is "against alcohol, for it almost ruined my life."

Case D

This person is involved with the American Indian Movement (AIM). A thirty-two-year-old Lakota male, he has stayed away from bars for a year and has not "been drinking for six months." In his capacity as a leader of AIM, he felt that he "was setting a bad example for his peers, younger people, and elders." His primary reason for abstinence, or at this stage, a tentative commitment not to imbibe alcohol, was personal. He was having marital problems and family discord in the *tiospaye* (extended family). He volunteered the information that his brief period of abstinence had "good after affects," and "being dry had a feeling of spiritual cleansing." His use of native religious forms, such as the sweat lodge (*Ini pi*), was not an Alcoholics Anonymous approach but "was our own." This person began drinking when he was about fourteen or fifteen years of age and in the eighth grade, while in attendance at a Bureau of Indian Affairs Boarding School.

Case E

This is an idiosyncratic case. He is a sixty-year-old Lakota male who has been sober for twelve years (1978). He left a Sioux reservation in 1963 and has been living in a city ever since. He began drinking in his early adolescence (at about seventeen years old) but did not become a steady drinker until his midtwenties. His life on the reservation was one of drinking, and he felt "dead about six months of the year." He attended an Alcoholics Anonymous program there and consulted a priest, as he was raised a Catholic. He did not fully understand the native Lakota religion. The old people "don't talk about it." He did meet one religious practitioner on the reservation and became very interested in seeking a native belief system. He became interested in tribal history and Lakota language. Five years ago he became very involved in the Sun Dance and *Yuwipi* ceremonies. He felt that he wanted to stay alive and see his children grow up. He felt that his schooling at a Bureau of Indian Affairs day school and boarding school, and a Catholic boarding school, deprived him of his native culture. The priests were constantly equating the native religion with superstitions and indicated that the only true faith was their own. Additionally, they expected great humility—as he stated, "one had to be on one's knees to the missionaries and the bureaucrats on the reservation." His father died in 1965 from cirrhosis of the liver. He decided then to stay away from the reservation and live in the city. But he felt that "there is something there (on the reservation), and it is more than roots." He is well aware of the suicide rates and violence, but he still feels strongly that "something is there." He recounted a variety of alcohol-related accidents that occurred to members of his extended family on the reservation. One male cousin was hit by a car, and the occupants "backed over—back and forth on him." There were no charges laid against the transgressors. Some of his drinking buddies suffocated; other relatives died in auto accidents. He was aware of what he labeled "self-destructive tendencies" on the part of young Lakota males. He felt that the idea of bravery was still important in how these males perceived themselves. He was one of the gangs that as "part of a warfare act" very often fought white males while drinking. This was "our idea of bravery—false courage," he stated. It was what he called *kola ki ya pi* (a traditional friendship group). He felt that the deprivation of culture that he encountered in his schooling was traumatic. After he sobered up, he usually felt that his actions were tied to some "search for identity."

He has attempted to adapt the four areas he knows—Christianity, Alcoholics Anonymous, counseling, and the native Lakota religion—into a meaningful mode of maintaining soberness. Indeed, he sees "an AA meeting as equivalent to a 'warrior society.'" He refers to verbalizing his conquering of "booze."

His own phenomenological system is interesting. He sees the Lakota Catlinite pipe as an important symbol of the Lakota nation. The *Ini pi* (sweat lodge) he sees as "a symbol of Mother Earth's womb." In it, he feels a "relaxation response, seclusion, a reenergizing force, communication with the Great Spirit in the six levels of the mind." Therefore, according to him, the six levels of the mind are "subconscious, conscious memory, creation, healing, intuition, and communication with the Great Spirit." The *Ini pi* "not only cleanses the body, but the mind." One concentrates on communion with the Great Spirit by thinking. One does not verbalize. "When one goes to an AA meeting, one verbalizes," he stated. He feels that his observation of counselors has taught him to be humble. He likens this to the Christian humility in which Jesus taught persons to humble themselves. He associates this humility with intercession in the Sun Dance, in which he was a participant. He stated, however, that he could not deal with a number of Christians who said, "You're just a dumb Indian." To meet their expected answer was to say, "Thank you." He was also aware of Carl Roger's client-centered therapy. He could not deal with "agendas" in an adequate manner. He felt that he could not keep silent if any Indian person became abusive and said, "Who the hell do you think you are, just because you quit drinking!"

He felt that awareness of an individual's history was important to maintain sobriety. In his case, he felt that if he "could deal with crises and maintain sobriety," he could continue in a maintenance pattern. He also indicated that it was "his spiritual experience in Indian ceremonies and not AA" that kept him sober. He told of an attempt at vision questing while he was hunting. This occurred in 1973, south of his natal community on the reservation. He offered a cigarette in four directions. He prayed to *Wakan Tanka* (Great Spirit), "I'm lost. Where are you? I want to know where to lean." Although it was damp and he was sitting on a rock, he felt a warmth and a calmness. He heard wind through the cottonwood trees and giant ants running in the grass. It was in December. He felt relieved and happy with a calmness he had never experienced at any AA meeting. The dryness and warmth symbolized for him that he was getting and maintaining sobriety and had "received it in the giving from *Wakan Tanka* and *Taku'skan'skan* (all things that move; invisible power). He thought carefully: "What do I change?" He used the native term, *Eglu zuzu epi* ("to take one's self apart"); he took "all the stress and anxiety of drinking" and quit drinking. Although he has lost friends, he has maintained sobriety. He feels that "alcohol is a trickster." This person has gone back to university and is hoping to work in the field of alcohol control among Indian groups in an urban area.

Cases F and G—Another Composite

These cases represent a married couple in their late forties. The man had been drinking most of his adult life. Not being a Lakota, but a person from another reservation, he experienced the tribal prejudice exhibited by some of the Lakota community members. It is reflected in this statement by one of his affines, "Those *sha glasha* (Chippewa or outsiders) have been notorious drinkers ever since some of them moved down here in their Red River carts." Thus, from a Lakota standpoint, he was fulfilling an expectation. It was, however, a great surprise when his Lakota wife joined him in periodic drinking binges. In 1976, they both came under the influence of Mormon missionaries and converted to Mormonism. They stopped drinking. They both became involved in the religious and social activities of the Mormons on the reservation and maintained sober states until 1979. The reasons for their mutual return to a drunken life were based upon marital discord.

During their tenure as abstainers, they elicited some criticism from the community—more particularly, their kinfolk. This couple became very judgmental about the drinking behavior of the rest of the group. They, especially the wife, issued mandates that no one could smoke or drink in her home. Rumors indicated that she had removed all ashtrays from her home. Thus, they were not visited and not included in kin and community events that were not Mormon centered. When they both succumbed to drink again, some *tiospaye* members were secretly pleased. "They thought they were too good for us, and thought they would never drink again," said a paternal aunt.

Case H—Still Another Coalescence

A fifty-six-year-old grandmother, this Lakota female began drinking when she was approximately twenty-five years old. She was precipitated into this action by the dissolution of a consensual marriage. She drank for about fifteen years and then joined the Mormon church. She has not imbibed since. She has compassion for drinkers, however. As she says, "I know what it's like; I used to drink, too." She has since devoted her life to the care of her grandchildren and foster children. Not only has this apparently given her direction in life, but the latter has also provided her with a means of income in uncertain reservation economics. She participates in the religious life of her new faith (she previously was a member of the Episcopal Church). She is also involved in community events and social activities, such as the school and the powwow, where she is primarily an observer. She states that she has no desire to start drinking again.

The other eight Lakota women who had drunk rather conspicuously and freely in their early years began to taper off in their forties. They then stopped drinking entirely, without any special aids. The aging factor has been a strong deterrent to drinking in these persons. Comments such as "I was old enough to know better," or "I was going to be a grandmother" were all reasons given for the assumption and continuation of sobriety. When asked if they felt that they would be tempted to imbibe alcohol again, most of them said that they "had gotten it out of their systems."

In a major community on the Standing Rock Reservation of 150 families—some are clustered in a newly designed housing unit of thirty new houses—there are approximately 200 adults. The outlying homes are included in the group. This follows the old *tiospaye* pattern. The season of the year and the time of the week are variables that affect whether or not fluctuation in the adult population is present. Employment is seasonal, and the men are away during the summer months. Women of all ages tend to be community bound and give the stability needed for the socialization of Sioux children. Therefore, one hears from women, "I don't drink," or "I drink but I'm not an alcoholic. I don't drink wine." It is generally conceded, however, that everyone drinks, which indicates that in this society, a nonjudgmental stance is operative. Reluctance to pinpoint someone as an alcoholic is evident.

These case studies reflect the cultural milieu in which they interacted as "drinkers" and continue to live as sober Sioux people. The cases are re-markable for the self-awareness that their move to sobriety engendered and for their perseverance to remain sober.

"I Got Tired of Drinking"
Interpretations of Intents and Continuities of Siouan Sober States

" I GOT TIRED OF DRINKING" is a recurrent theme throughout many of the cases and is given by Lakota persons as a reason to stop drinking alcohol. This statement in English is a direct translation from the Lakota term *ta watl yesni*, which was elicited by two psychologists on Standing Rock Reservation (Johnson and Johnson 1965). They interpret it to signify being "totally discouraged." The native term is more appropriately translated as "tiredness" of an obnoxious situation or as "approaching with dread." Placed in contextual frames of alcohol use, this can be interpreted either in Lakota or in reservation English as simply deploring a situation—in this case, the life of drinking alcohol. Rejecting a life of dissonance and dissipation owing to drinking and attempting to assume a more productive life are at the base of this process. This is strikingly apparent in the case studies.

The main thrust of my research has been to isolate the matrix of purposive action articulated and evidenced by the sobriety seekers. How do Sioux Indians restructure a defensible self-image after a long period of alcohol use and abuse? That is the major question. Braroe (1975), writing about the Cree of Canada, noted,

> Feeling guilty for transgressing a moral rule is not the same as being guilty. One feels guilty when one's action is felt as a blemish on the inner self, when one has violated standards that are accepted as part of one's own moral worth. Obviously, Indians do not experience the guilt that whites associate with their own drinking and readily use to evaluate Indians' drinking. There is one very revealing exception to this pattern. During the Sun Dance liquor is forbidden, and no one present in the circle of tents around

the sacred lodge may possess or consume it. This rule is observed and enforced by the majority of the band; and the few who break it are scolded,
a sanction apparently strong enough to dissuade infractions by most of the
community. This is the sole occasion on which drinking appears to be a
source of guilt on the reserve. When asked why alcohol was forbidden at
this time and at no other, an Indian man replied positively: "Because the
Sun Dance is an Indian thing and drinking is a white thing." (141)

Seldom in the literature on alcohol use in the northern Plains is there such
a strong contextual flavor as Braroe gives here. It indicates a compartmental-
ization that allows Indians to coexist with non-Indians in separate socioeconomic and ritual spheres. Moreover, the description imparts a biculturalism
that is normative in the Plains area and pervasive in Lakota life.

It is apparent that guilt or shame is not an effective mode of discourag-
ing Lakota drinkers. It seems obvious in the case studies presented that a
period of self-assessment and a reevaluation of directions in one's life was
necessary. Although Levy and Kunitz (1974) attribute a lack of introspection to the Navajo male drinker, they nevertheless indicate that many
Navajo men stop drinking at middle age and do it without difficulty or apparent external coercion. They write: "Aging itself causes a cutting down
of drinking [among the Navajo.] In any event, the high proportion of
Navajo males who have quit after years of heavy drinking leads us to question the chronic addictive nature of 'Indian alcoholism'" (137).

Aging does not seem to be as important a variable in Siouan sobriety,
although it has some relevance. In fact, there are at least three women who
began to drink for the first time in their lives in their late fifties and early
sixties. This was unusual, however, and was tied to loss of close kinspersons. As for the Lakota males, many continue drinking to the very end of
their lives. There is no great censure directed at these aged drinkers. Some
community members say, "Well, they have nothing to look forward to."
Again, this reflects the norm of the individualism, and the lack of stringent
social control.

Therefore, the assumption of a sober state as a new way of life is a
highly idiosyncratic act for Lakota individuals. Withdrawing from the
world of drink on all Lakota reservations and social groups is a very painful
process. Peer pressure is extremely intense, with social isolation being the
price one must pay for sobriety. Extreme pressure is applied to force persons to begin drinking again. A reformed drinker mentioned that the
"hardest part of being sober is the loss of my friends." Courage and a cer-

tain self-isolation seem in order for the maintenance of sobriety. Being a social isolate is not a desirable role for any Lakota.

Social pressures exerted upon any Indian person who wishes to maintain a sober state are great. Lang (1979) specifically mentions them for urban Chippewa males. MacGregor (1945) and Kemnitzer (1972) indicate a "leveling process" that attempts to pull down all Sioux persons who rise to the higher levels of reservation hierarchies—socially, educationally, or economically. This process among the Sioux is slightly different from the "leveling process" often described in such alcohol prevention programs as Alcoholics Anonymous (AA) where leveling is a means of making the drunkard seeking reform a member of a supportive group. Sadler (1979) notes that "such leveling is of practical significance to members who assert that despair and elation are equally dangerous to sobriety" (392). Rather than being supportive as in the reformative movement of AA, Lakota leveling is often punitive and destructive. Such statements as "You're too good to drink with us," "You're not a Lakota anymore," "You think you are white now," and others are equally damaging and frequently evoked to put someone down. These are powerful statements used to alter the sober stance of Lakota persons and to topple a person from a resolve to remain in a state of abstinence. Pressures to belong are still very important in the egalitarian nature of this social group in which individual identity as a Lakota person is embedded. This can be an almost unbearable burden for an individual and almost necessitates an isolationist position in a social system in which identity is tied to *tiospaye* and tribe.

It is apparent from the various studies on Sioux Indian drinking that intoxication provides a temporary relief from the conflicts and anxieties of daily life (Kemnitzer 1972; Maynard 1969; Prager 1972; Whittaker 1962, 1963). Yet, the imbibing of alcohol does not fully resolve these uncertainties. It seems clear that attempting sobriety is seen as a means of establishing and maintaining a means of resolving conflicts in one's life. Actual and constructive efforts to effect a changed behavior and alter the course of one's life do occur. Continuously sober persons need to reorganize their life pattern and interpersonal relationships to sustain themselves in an ongoing quest for a life free from alcohol. This is not an easy road.

In the case studies, one is struck with the increased self-awareness formed as part of the process for change. A new identity with an enhanced self-image seems to have been forged from the rubble of alcohol addiction. The attempt to build a new way of life not based upon drinking is a dramatic process for these individuals.

The introspection that Levy and Kunitz note as lacking among the Navajo males seems to be a feature of Lakota male decision making. The procedure of thinking things over appears to be significant in the quest of sober behavior. This process is glossed by a native term *ah bleza* ("to examine") or another which is *ah bluk'h chanki* ("to think through carefully" or "to ponder"). When one consults a native practitioner for help in dealing with stresses and uncertainties, or if one wishes to change one's way of living, one is asked to *ah bleza*, "to examine," one's actions. By carefully weighing one's behavior and seeing one's mistakes it is then possible to assume a different way of living. Many Lakota persons who are not fluent in the native language often refer to this process as exhibiting willpower. This phrase is the most often evoked by others to explain the continued sobriety of former drinkers. Whittaker (1962, 1963) also mentions the term in this context.

Unfortunately, the literature on Indian alcoholism often reinforces the popular image that drinking is an all-consuming activity for most Indians. The very nature of the economic system militates against the constant utilization of alcohol. It has been established in other studies (Hurt and Brown 1965; Kemnitzer 1972; Maynard 1969; Whittaker 1963; White 1970) that there are periods, particularly at the beginning of each month, at which a noticeable increase in Sioux drinking occurs. This, then, gives an economic basis for temporary abstinence patterns. Satisfying the demand is limited by lack of income.

There are, moreover, specific times when Lakota people do not imbibe. Religious events, whether native or Christian, are times when sobriety prevails. Other periods of sobriety occur during certain rites, such as naming ceremonies, birthing times, or funerals and memorial feasts. Any untoward drinking is certain to bring censure upon the offenders by the *tiospaye* members and gossip from the community. Men never drink when hunting. Many of the more traditional men utilize charms and certain roots during this event, and liquor is forbidden. The prevailing pattern of white behavior is assumed by the more acculturated when fishing. Men, and sometimes women, drink beer during this activity. Utilization of alcohol is exceedingly prevalent at rodeos where whites and Indians interact. This appears to be a pattern in the northern Plains (Braroe 1975). Drinking, though often officially banned, is becoming common at powwows. These are largely social events on the reservations and in urban areas. As is common in the larger society, alcoholic beverages are now assuming prominence at birthdays for adults, weddings, and divorces.

The Sun Dance was revived in 1953 and has proliferated since 1969. It has not been completely analyzed as a revitalization movement. Its long-term impact on alcoholism has not yet been assessed. The revived Sun Dance ritual and other older ceremonies, such as the *Yuwipi*, which is a curing ceremony, forbid the presence of anyone who has used alcohol. The smoking of anything (specifically *pezi*, which translates as "grass") except the sacred tobacco is also proscribed. These rules are strictly enforced, and anyone with a suspicious odor—even of perfume—is usually turned away from the ceremony. Participants in these ceremonies are ideally not allowed to drink alcohol. But in their daily lives away from the seasonal ritual event, this is not and cannot be enforced. There are instances in which many of the newly emerging medicine men have been intoxicated on their speaking tours to universities or in their lives on reservations. Again, this reflects Lakota individualism and lack of censure. Gossip is not an all-powering control mechanism.

It is obvious, however, that some persons participate in the Sun Dance for therapeutic reasons, as persons of Lakota heritage do, to seek personal transformation. The search for supernatural aid to eliminate dependence upon an intrusive and abusive item—alcohol—is a new departure in the ritual. This is a variant from the previous function, which was the preservation of the social order. Participation was then primarily for the welfare of the group. This buttresses Jorgenson's (1972) analysis of the Sun Dance of the Ute and Shoshone, which was seen by the participants of many tribes as an alternative to drinking and a possible means of achieving rigorous temperance.

Long-range evaluation of the effects of participation in the Sun Dance as a control measure for alcohol prevention was not possible in 1980. The episodic nature of the event (summertime) indicates that it does not supply a continuous support system for those persons who dance to desist from drinking. Some religious practitioners do not imbibe at all. These are usually the older ritualists. One leader of the Sun Dance on Standing Rock began to drink heavily after the death of his oldest son, whose death was drug related. He has been criticized by some members of his community. Others feel much compassion because of the unfortunate death of his son. He still participates in naming ceremonies and rituals of the dead, and he is gradually resuming his role in Sun Dance preparations.

The Sun Dance serves to provide prestige and honor in participating, status in scarification marks, compassion for the people offering prayers, and enhanced Indian identity for the contemporary Indian male. Besides, sun dancing enters into the arena as a means of controlling excessive use of alcohol. The rite has now spread to Siouan groups in Canada. A revitalized ritual, the Sun Dance is not completely integrated into the contemporary symbolic belief structure of the Sioux, as yet. As a previously repressed religion, with the underlying basic structure of native language and value systems also suppressed, complete integration and manifestation of belief is still being formulated—especially on an individual level. Increasingly the Sun Dance is becoming a Pan-Indian/intertribal phenomenon, with other tribes—Shoshone, Cree, Micmac, Blood, Canadian Dakota, and others—also seeking enlightenment in a native faith. Moreover, the Sun Dance is a regularized event performed on an annual basis, occurring at various places on the Sioux reservations during the summer months. Though intense and evocative of deep religious feelings, the rite is not of sufficient duration to have lasting effects as an alcohol-control mechanism. Participants come from different Sioux reservations, and there is little *espirit de corps* or continual intensification. There is no sustained support system that might function through the year in isolated Lakota communities or in urban areas.

Some Lakota—again, most often males—attend the *Yuwipi* ceremony as a means of obtaining help for their drinking problems. Though this is primarily a curing or clairvoyance ceremony, depending upon the wishes of the initiator or patient, there are reasons for its performance. Participants in the ritual, besides the patient, ask for help by supplicating and imploring the *Wakan Tanka* (Great Spirit) and supernatural spirits. Kemnitzer (1978), in reference to the Oglala Sioux, indicates, "Others also ask for help; people who had lost things, people giving thanks for previous help, men worried about a wife's illness, and women worried about their husband's drinking" (3). A *Yuwipi* ceremony may be held specifically for a person who has a drinking problem. This is usually activated by his parents, wife, or members of his kin group. All persons present meditate on his problem and pray for him. However, if the ceremony is held for drinking control or anything else, any person present may ask the supernatural spirits for aid to curb his drinking problem. There is no evidence that anyone has been cured through this rite. It is, nonetheless, the only indigenous support system beside the Sun Dance and the *Ini pi* or purifying sweat lodge that is associated with both of the other ceremonies. Many persons attend the *Yuwipi* to call attention to the fact that they are cognizant of their drinking problems. The religious practitioner does not assume any part of a treatment modality for the person who publicly acknowledges his affinity for alcohol. He merely requests supernatural aid.

Attending the *Yuwipi* and participating in the sweat lodge (*Ini pi*)—now called colloquially "sweat"—has increased as an alcohol-control mechanism (Kemnitzer 1972).

When individuals of either sex seek aid from a religious practitioner or native counselor, the person does not receive stringent directions for change. Participants are simply asked to *ah bleza* (examine) their actions and implement change. There is strong emphasis on *chin k'a cha* (individual autonomy) and reason and will to change. The therapist listens and may give advice in a nonthreatening, nonjudgmental manner.

It is generally conceded in the ethnographic literature (Erikson 1960; Goldfrank 1943; Hassrick 1961; Lee 1959; MacGregor 1945) that Lakota culture evidenced weak social and psychological controls upon the individuals, particularly males. Coming from a nomadic hunting and gathering economy, a certain independence of thought and action was important in the behavior of males, who earned prestige through individual effort and achievement. Masculine striving and accomplishment were fulfilled through the vision quest, prowess in the hunt, and self-glorification through mutilation in the Sun Dance—these actions were basic to the acknowledged *bloka* (male superiority) nature of Lakota maleness. If one accepts the postulate advocated by such writers as George and Louise Spindler (1957, 1978) and Hallowell (1955) that residual personality traits are important components of contemporary Indian identities, one can readily comprehend the individualistic nature of the Lakota person. An interesting correlation is found in a cross-cultural study of Sioux children (Havighurst and Neugarten 1955), which indicates that moral surrogates who evaluate behavior of the Sioux boys mentioned male age mates more frequently than the girls. The finding strongly suggests the power of the peer group that has been mentioned repeatedly in many studies of Siouan drunkenness (Kemnitzer 1972, 1978; Maynard 1969; Prager 1972; Whittaker 1962, 1963; and others). Further, indications are that peer pressure is exerted early in life, as the children studied were from age eight onward to ten. The situation may be further exacerbated by the isolation of reservations as social enclaves, where adolescent interaction is principally with others of the same ethnic group, and mostly with one's kin group. Of even greater importance is the fact that many Sioux children are products of boarding schools—Bureau of Indian Affairs and parochial—where role models of parents were lacking, and few effective authority figures set standards of behavior.

Contemporary Lakota Sioux society, which forms the backdrop to drinking alcohol and for choosing sobriety, has remained egalitarian in ethos and orientation. Within the drinking rubric, the sharing ethic predominates for both males and females. The ethos is an ideology that is solidly based in the socialization process and is firmly entrenched in the value system of present-day Lakota people. This worldview is the essence of being a Lakota person.

Though not seen as an attribute by the administrators of the various government agencies, sharing has allowed for cultural and economic survival in an unfavorable ecological niche. The cultural value has been a necessity in all phases of living—and has been an important fact in the arena of alcohol use. Orientation to the present might be an explanation for the hedonistic character of Lakota drinking.

It is difficult to overestimate the economic deprivation that has been the lot of the Sioux and other tribes of the northern Plains, which is well documented (MacGregor 1945; Maynard and Twiss 1970; Schusky 1975; Useem and Eicher 1970). The flexibility and pooling of kin (*tiospaye*) for labor and income have allowed the Lakota to exist in a marginal situation. Mutual but unspecified reciprocities have given the Lakota capabilities to cope with chronic and ongoing socioeconomic deprivation. Though recognizing a Lakota individualism, a Lakota collectivism has been predominant and has exerted a stringent but subtle tether to prevent many persons from seeking sobriety as a completely satisfying way of life.

Summary and Conclusions
"There's a Lot to Drinking"

THE ABOVE QUOTE IS FROM a forty-year-old Lakota Sioux male who had stopped drinking after imbibing for thirty years. It seems a fitting adage to remember when attempting a summary of a complex situation involving alcohol use that has been the lot of many Indians for several generations.

A first conclusion of this study is that the term "alcoholism," which is culture bound, is not greatly applicable to the Sioux, nor to other tribal groups. Tribes differ in their histories of contact, worldviews, patterns of behavior, and use of alcohol. Adaptations to new cultural forms and behavioral patterns have been unique and functional in their terms.

With the Lakota Sioux there appears to be some hesitancy to label other members of the group, but the term "drinking" is used to cover an entire gamut of drinking habits, styles, and behaviors. The white concept of alcoholic has assumed some relevancy since the 1960s with the impact of federal programs that provide a funding base for alleviation of alcohol-related problems. The term "alcoholic" began to be used to pinpoint *any* person of Lakota heritage who drinks alcohol. Alcohol prevention programs are seen as supplemental to a scarce employment situation, and funds are used for problem amelioration but mainly for economic gain.

As for the drinking styles of the Lakota Sioux, one can offer some generalizations. Alcohol was traded to these tribal bands at the time of contact with Europeans. Alcohol was undoubtedly sought as a new mind-altering experience that fit into a visionary complex of traditional Sioux culture. But for the European, it was part of a mercantile economy with a profit motive.

The placement of Sioux upon reservations with continuous legal restrictions upon the sale of liquor contributed to their development of a sporadic drinking style. This style was characterized by intense and quick consumption until all the liquor was consumed. Resultant behavior was flamboyant and unpredictable. This manner of drinking was a protective measure predicated upon the illegality of having liquor and the necessity to consume any evidence. Bootleggers were white in those early days, but at present some Lakota persons—male and female—who have obtained sobriety, act as middle persons. Many are underwritten by local liquor stores whose owners are non-Indians. These facts indicate that economic concerns have been ongoing since the days of early Indian-white contact. The symbiotic nature of interethnic interaction among many Plains Indian groups remains economic.

The important features of Lakota Sioux drinking patterns might be summarized as:

1. Drinking alcohol is a common feature of life on Sioux reservations or where Sioux congregate in urban areas. Imbibing of alcoholic beverages might be seen as a characteristic act in contemporary Lakota life.
2. Children grow up to adulthood in a cultural milieu that fosters drinking via role models.
3. By age fifteen, most Lakota males have tasted alcohol, and some are drinking on a regular basis.
4. Women, though not so obsessed with alcohol use, have been drinking more extensively since 1955.
5. Heavy drinkers among Lakota males outnumber similar drinkers among females by a rough estimate of three to one.
6. The peak of alcohol use for Lakota males is from approximately twenty-one to thirty-six years of age. This age period also correlates with the greatest acts of daring—aggressive acts toward both the out-group and the in-group, automobile accidents, suicides, and homicides.
7. There is a marked decline in drinking among women in their early forties. This is mirrored in some men who attempt to stop drinking at approximately the same age. Peer group pressure to continue drinking is exceedingly strong for Lakota males.
8. There are only a few total abstainers in Lakota Sioux society since the lifting of prohibition in 1953. Those who have never used alcohol tend to be older women.

Lakota persons evidence high visibility due to racial characteristics, styles of clothing, and demeanor. Drinking is of a public nature. Sporadic binge drinking is a generalized pattern with periods of abstinence of varying lengths. The availability of money in the extended family (*tiospaye*) or male friendship group (*Kola ki ya pi*) generally determines whether or not alcohol is consumed. The Siouan sharing syndrome is ubiquitous and is critical in understanding the strength of the peer group in Lakota drinking behavior.

In some respects, Lakota drinking can be said to have some positive functions. A basic one is an Indian (Lakota) identity, sharing, social cohesion, increased social interaction in conviviality, and feelings of power—both social and physical. These are important elements in an ecological region where racism and economic deprivation are parts of Lakota daily life.

The negative aspects of Lakota Sioux drinking can be seen in the abuse of alcohol, with resultant social disorders such as ill health, accidental death, occasional murders, injury and assault, and frequently, theft. In the realm of the *tiospaye*, dissonance and kin discord, unemployment with undue stress on productive members, divorce, and neglect and abuse of parents, spouses, and children are significant factors.

Though Lakota Sioux people do not see the use of alcohol as an aspect of deviance in their communities, the dissonance caused by its excessive use is noted. The impact of alcohol treatment programs and the resultant changed perceptions are emerging. Revitalization of Lakota belief and ritual is also a factor, which may be more ameliorative. As the label of "alcoholic" is now being applied to some persons, so is their growing awareness of the debilitating effects of excessive and indiscriminate use of alcoholic beverages. Awareness and personal decisions have led some Lakota persons to deliberately seek a continual state of sobriety.

Factors to be considered in this new search for sobriety include the following:

1. No strong internal controls have been developed in the indigenous society to control excessive drinking, for drinking is not seen as a problem to most Lakota Sioux.
2. An ethic of concern is surfacing. At present, it is idiosyncratic and individual, which reflects the general individualistic tenor of the society. It is from these individuals that a thrust to sobriety is being attempted.
3. The revitalization of native beliefs, such as the Sun Dance, so long legally suppressed, is an attempt at establishing an ethic and ideology that would motivate Siouan persons to confront the social

ills of contemporary life, especially alcohol abuse. Such an accomplishment would foster a more meaningful and purposive life. At present, no charismatic leader has arisen to coalesce the doctrine, as in the case of the Code of Handsome Lake.

4. As a corollary to achieving sobriety through a native ritual, some persons have utilized a more stable economic base to maintain the status of being a Sioux. Further, the maintenance of sobriety has been helped through educational endeavors or in alcohol-related work.

A final statement regarding the difficulties for Lakota Sioux people in achieving and maintaining sobriety is that many view their behavior as definitely being one response to externally imposed circumstances and policies. This view results partly from the fact that for generations human relationships among them have been externally administered. When Lakota see their behaviors as internally motivated and personal, as is the case with the few who have attained a permanent state of sobriety, then new behavioral norms might be engendered, effected, and transformed into socialization patterns. However, a more critical and overarching constraint is the Lakota Sioux reluctance to pressure others into specific patterns of behavior that would compel the individual to become a social isolate. Lakota group identity is a valued sentiment. While "there is a lot to drinking," it is "a rough road to staying sober."

References

Aberle, D. F. 1966. *The peyote religion among the Navajo*. Chicago: Aldine.

Ablon, J. 1964. Relocated American Indians in the San Francisco Bay area: Social interactions and Indian identity. *Human Organization* 23 (4): 296–304.

———. 1965. American Indian relocation: Problems of dependency and management in the city. *Phylon* 26:362–71.

———. 1971. Cultural conflicts in urban Indians. *Mental Hygiene* 55 (2): 199–205.

———. 1975. Research frontiers for anthropologists in family studies, a case in point: Alcoholism and the family. *Human Organization* 38 (2): 196–200.

Adair, J. 1930. *Adair's history of the American Indians*, ed. S. C. Williams. New York: Promontory Press.

American Indian Policy Review Commission. 1977. *Final report*. Washington, D.C.: U.S. Government Printing Office.

Bacon, M. K., H. Barry III, and I. L. Child. 1965. A cross-cultural study of drinking, II: Relations to other features of culture. *Quarterly Journal of Studies on Alcohol*, supplement 3, 29–48.

Barnouw, V. 1950. *Acculturation and personality among the Wisconsin Chippewa*. Memoir of the American Anthropological Association.

Barter, E. R., and J. T. Barter. 1974. Urban Indians and mental health problems. *Psychiatric Annals* 4 (11): 37–43.

Basso, K. M. 1966. *The gift of Changing Woman* (Bulletin 196, Bureau of American Ethnology, 76, 113–73). Washington, D.C.: U.S. Government Printing Office.

———. 1970. *The Cibecue Apache*. New York: Holt, Rinehart and Winston.

Becker, E. 1973. *The denial of death*. New York: Free Press.

Beiser, M. 1974. Indian mental health. *Psychiatric Annals* 4 (9): 3–5.

Bennett, J. W. 1969. *Northern plainsmen*. Chicago: Aldine.

Bennion, L. J., and T. K. Li. 1976. Alcohol metabolism in American Indians and whites. *New England Journal of Medicine* 284:9–13.

Bharati, A. 1974. Anthropological approaches to the study of religion: Ritual belief systems. In *Biennial review of anthropology*, vol. 7, ed. B. J. Siegel, 230–82. Stanford, Calif.: Stanford University Press.

Bishop, C. A. 1974. *The northern Ojibwa and the fur trade: An historical and ecological study*. Toronto: Holt, Rinehart and Winston of Canada.

Blakeslee, C. 1955. Some observations on the Indians of Crow Creek reservation, South Dakota. *Plains Anthropologist* 5:31–35.

Bourke, J. G. 1894. Distillation by early American Indians. *American Anthropologist* 7 (3): 297–99.

Boyer, L. B. 1964. Folk psychiatry of the Apache of the Mescalero Indian reservation. In *Magic, faith, and healing: Studies in primitive psychiatry today*, ed. A. Kiev, 384–419. New York: Free Press.

Boyer, R. M. 1964. The matrifocal family among the Mescalero: Additional dats. *American Anthropologist* 66:593–602.

Braroe, N. W. 1975. *Indian and white*. Stanford, Calif.: Stanford University Press.

Bunzel, R. 1940. The role of alcoholism in two central American cultures. *Psychiatry* 3:361–87.

———. 1976. Chamula and Chichicastenango: A reassessment. In *Cross-cultural approaches to the study of alcohol*, ed. M. W. Everett, J. O. Waddell, and D. B. Heath, 21–22. The Hague, Netherlands: Mouton.

Bynam, J. 1972. Suicide and the American Indian: An analysis of recent trends. In *Native Americans today: Sociological perspectives*, ed. H. M. Bahr, B. A. Chadwick, and R. C. Day, 364–97. New York: Harper & Row.

Carpenter, E. S. 1959. Alcohol in the Iroquois dream quest. *American Journal of Psychiatry* 116:148–51.

Castile, G. F. 1974. Federal Indian policy and the sustained enclave: An anthropological perspective. *Human Organization* 33 (3): 219–28.

Chittenden, H. M. 1902. *The American fur trade of the far west*. New York: Frances P. Harper.

Coffey, T. G. 1966. Problem drinking among American Indians. *Journal of Studies on Alcohol, Inc. Alcoholism Treatment Digest*, 12–15. New Brunswick, N.J.

Cohen, F. S. 1942. *Handbook of federal Indian law*. Washington, D.C.: U.S. Department of the Interior. Reprinted, Albuquerque: University of New Mexico Press, 1974.

Cooley, R. 1980. Alcoholism programs. In *Drinking behavior among southwestern Indians*, ed. J. O. Waddell and M. W. Everett. Tucson: University of Arizona Press.

Curlee, W. V. 1969. Suicide and self-destructive behavior on the Cheyenne River reservation. In *Suicide among the American Indians* (Publication No. 1908, June), 34–36. Washington, D.C.: U.S. Public Health Service.

Curley, R. T. 1967. Drinking patterns of the Mescalero Apache. *Quarterly Journal of Studies on Alcohol* 28 (1): 116–31.

Daniels, R. E. 1970. Cultural identities among the Oglala Sioux. In *The modern Sioux*, ed. E. Nurge, 198–245. Lincoln: University of Nebraska Press.

Debo, A. 1970. *A history of Indians of the United States.* Norman: University of Oklahoma Press.

Deloria, E. C. 1945. *Speaking of Indians.* New York: Friendship Press. Reprinted, Vermillion, S.Dak.: Dakota Press, 1979.

Deloria, V., Jr. 1969. *Custer died for your sins.* New York: MacMillan.

———. 1970. *We Talk, You Listen: New Tribes, New Turf.* New York: MacMillan.

Denig, E. T. 1930. Indian tribes of the upper Missouri. In *Forty-sixth Annual Report,* ed. J. N. B. Hewitt, 375–628. Washington, D.C.: Bureau of American Ethnology.

———. 1961. *Five Indian tribes of the upper Missouri: Sioux, Arickaras, Assiniboines, Crees, Crows,* ed. J. C. Ewers. Norman: University of Oklahoma Press.

Devereux, G. 1948. The function of alcohol in Mohave society. *Quarterly Journal of Studies on Alcohol* 9 (2): 207–51.

Dosman, E. J. 1972. *Indians: The urban dilemma.* Toronto: McClelland Stewart.

Dozier, E. P. 1966. Problem drinking among American Indians: The role of socio-cultural deprivation. *Quarterly Journal of Studies on Alcohol* 27:72–87.

Driver, H. E. 1955. Alcoholic beverages in native North America. *Proceedings of the Indiana Academy of Science,* 50–51.

———. 1961. *Indians of North America.* Chicago: University of Chicago Press.

Driver, H. E., and W. C. Massey. 1957. Comparative studies of North American Indians, 8: Narcotics and stimulants. *Transactions of the American Philosophical Society* 2:260–75.

Dyck, L. E. 1986. Are North American Indians biochemically more susceptible to the effects of alcohol? *Native Studies Review* 2:85–95.

Dyer, D. T. 1969. Human problems in an Indian culture. *Family Coordinator* 4:332–25.

Erikson, E. H. 1939. Observations on Sioux education. *The Journal of Psychology* 7:101–56.

———. 1960. *Childhood and society.* New York: W. W. Norton.

Everett, M. W. 1970. Pathology in White Mountain Apache culture: A preliminary analysis. *Western Canadian Journal of Anthropology* 2 (1): 180–203.

———. 1980. Drinking as a measure of proper behavior: The White Mountain Apaches. In *Drinking behavior among southwestern Indians,* ed. J. O. Waddell and M. Everett, 148–77. Tucson: University of Arizona Press.

Everett, M. W., J. O. Waddell, and D. B. Heath, eds. 1976. *Cross cultural approaches to the study of alcohol.* The Hague, Netherlands: Mouton.

Federal and State Indian Reservations. 1971. An EDA Handbook. Washington, D.C.: U.S. Government Printing Office.

Fenna, D. L., L. Mix, O. Schaefer, and J. A. Gilbert. 1971. Ethanol metabolism in various racial groups. *Canadian Medical Association Journal* 105 (5): 472–75. Reprinted in *Cross-cultural approaches to the study of alcohol,* ed. M. W. Everett, J. O. Waddell, and D. B. Heath, 227–34. The Hague, Netherlands: Mouton, 1978.

Ferguson, F. N. 1966. The peer group and Navajo problem drinking. Unpublished paper read at the 1st Annual Meeting of the Southern Anthropological Society.

———. 1968. Navajo drinking: Some tentative hypotheses. *Human Organization* 27:159–67.

———. 1970. Treatment program for Navajo alcoholics: Results after four years. *Quarterly Journal of Studies on Alcohol* 31:898–919.

———. 1976a. Stake theory as an explanatory device in Navajo alcohol treatment response. *Human Organization* 35 (1): 65–77.

———. 1976b. Similarities and differences among a heavily arrested group of Navajo Indian drinkers in a southwestern Indian town. In *Cross-cultural approaches to the study of alcohol*, ed. M. W. Everett, J. D. Waddell, and D. B. Heath, 161–71. The Hague, Netherlands: Mouton.

Field, P. B. 1962. A new cross-cultural study of drunkenness. In *Society, culture, and drinking*, ed. D. J. Pittman and C. R. Snyder, 48–74. New York: John Wiley.

Flannery, R. 1932. The position of women among the Mescalero Apache. *Primitive Man* 5:26–32.

Frederick, C. 1973. *Suicide, homicide and alcoholism among American Indians.* Washington, D.C.: National Institute of Mental Health Publication.

Gaalswyck, J. R. 1979. Teton Dakota beliefs about health and illness problems of their children: An exploratory study. Unpublished master's thesis. University of Washington, School of Nursing, Seattle, Wash.

Goldfrank, E. S. 1943. Historic change and social character: A study of the Teton Dakota. *American Anthropologist* 45:306–21.

Graves, T. D. 1967. Acculturation, access and alcoholism in a tri-ethnic community. *American Anthropologist* 69:302–21.

———. 1970. The personal adjustment of Navajo Indian migrants to Denver, Colorado. *American Anthropologist* 72:35–54.

———. 1971. Drinking and drunkenness among urban Indians. In *The American Indian in urban society*, ed. J. D. Waddell and O. M. Watsons, 274–311. Boston: Little, Brown.

Grobsmith, E. 1974. Wakunza: Use of Yuwipi medicine power in contemporary Teton Dakota culture. *Plains Anthropologist* 19:129–33.

———. 1981. *Lakota of the Rosebud: A contemporary ethnography.* New York: Holt, Rinehart and Winston.

Hackenburg, R. A., and M. M. Gallagher. 1972. The costs of cultural change: Accidental injury and modernization among the Papago Indians. *Human Organization* 31:211–26.

Hafen, B. Q. 1977. *Alcohol: The crutch that cripples.* St. Paul, Minn.: West Publishing Company.

Hallowell, A. I. 1955. *Culture and experience.* Philadelphia: University of Pennsylvania Press.

Hamer, J. H., and J. Steinberg. 1980. *Alcohol and native peoples of the north*. Lanham, Md.: University Press of America.

Hamer, J. M. 1965. Acculturation stress and the functions of alcohol among the Forest Potawatomi. *Quarterly Journal of Studies on Alcohol* 26:285–303.

———. 1969. Guardian spirits, alcohol, and cultural defense mechanisms. *Anthropologica* 11:215–41.

Hanna, J. M. 1976. Ethnic groups, human variation, and alcohol use. In *Cross-cultural approaches to the study of alcohol*, ed. M. W. Everett, J. O. Waddell, and D. B. Heath, 235–42. The Hague, Netherlands: Mouton.

Hannerz, U. 1969. *Soulside: Inquires into ghetto culture and community*. New York: Columbia University Press.

Hara, H. S. 1980. *The Hare Indians and their world*. Ottawa: National Museum of Man, Mercury Series Canadian Ethnology Service, Paper No. 63.

Hassrick, R. B. 1961. *The Sioux*. Norman: University of Oklahoma Press.

Havighurst, R. J., and B. Neugarten. 1955. *American Indian and white children: A sociopsychological investigation*. Chicago: University of Chicago Press.

Heath, D. B. 1981. Determining the sociocultural context of alcohol use. *Journal of Studies on Alcohol*, supplement 9, 9–17.

Hickerson, H. 1956. The genesis of a trading post band: The Pembina Chippewa. *Ethnohistory* 3 (4): 289–345.

Hoffman, H., and A. A. Noem. 1975. Alcohol and abstinence among relatives of American Indian alcoholics. *Journal of Studies in Alcohol* 1:165.

Honigmann, J. J. 1965. Social disintegration in the northern communities. *Canadian Review of Sociology and Anthropology* 4:119–214.

Honigmann, J. J., and I. Honigmann. 1945. Drinking in an Indian-white community. *Quarterly Journal of Studies on Alcohol* 4:575–619.

———. 1970. *Arctic townsmen: Ethnic backgrounds and modernization*, 97–107. Ottawa: Canadian Research Center for Anthropology, St. Paul University.

Hopen, E. C. 1964. A note on Alkali Fulfulde: A reformative movement among the nomadic Fulbe (Fulani) in Sokot Province. *Africa* 34:21–27.

Hornby, R., and R. H. Dana Jr., eds. 1984. *Mni Wakan and the Sioux: Respite, release, and recreation*. Brandon, Manitoba: Justin Publishing Company.

Horton, D. D. 1943. The function of alcohol in primitive societies: A cross-cultural study. *Quarterly Journal of Studies on Alcohol* 4:199–320.

Howard, J. 1979. *The British Museum winter count* (Occasional paper no. 4). London: British Museum.

Hurt, W. R. 1961. The urbanization of the Yankton Sioux. *Human Organization* 20 (4): 226–31.

Hurt, W. R., and R. M. Brown. 1965. Social drinking patterns of the Yankton Sioux. *Human Organization* 24:157–69.

Hyde, G. E. 1937. *Red Cloud's folk: A history of the Oglala Sioux*. Norman: University of Oklahoma Press.

———. 1961. *Spotted Tail's folk: A history of the Brule Sioux.* Norman: University of Oklahoma Press.

Indian Health Service. 1977. *Alcoholism: A high priority health problem.* Task Force on Indian Alcoholism. Washington, D.C.: U.S. Government Printing Office.

Jellinek, E. M. 1952. Phases of alcohol addiction. *Quarterly Journal of Studies in Alcohol* 13:673–84.

Jilek-Aall, L. 1974. Psychological aspects of drinking among Coast Salish Indians. *Canadian Psychiatric Association Journal* 4:357–61.

Johnson, D. L., and C. A. Johnson. 1965. Totally discouraged: A depressive syndrome among the Sioux. *Transcultural Psychiatric Research* 11:141–43.

Johnson, W. E. 1917. *The federal government and the liquor traffic.* Westerville, Ohio: American Issue Publishing Company.

Jorgenson, J. G. 1971. Indians and the metropolis. In *The American Indian in urban society,* ed. J. O. Waddell and O. M. Watson, 66–113. Boston: Little, Brown.

———. 1972. *The Sun Dance religion: Power for the powerless.* Chicago: University of Chicago Press.

Joseph, A., R. B. Spicer, and J. Chesky. 1945. *The desert people.* Chicago: University of Chicago Press.

Jules-Rosette, B. 1978. The veil of objectivity: Prophecy, divination, and social inquiry. *American Anthropologist* 80 (3): 549–70.

Kemnitzer, L. S. 1972. The structure of country drinking parties on the Pine Ridge reservation, South Dakota. *Plains Anthropologist* 17:134–42.

———. 1976. Structure, content, and cultural meaning of Yuwipi: A modern Lakota healing rite. *American Ethnologist* 3:261–80.

———. 1978. "Yuwipi." *Indian Historian* 11 (2): 2–5.

Kopytoff, I. 1964. Classifications of religious movements: Analytical and synthetic. In *Symposium on new approaches to the study of religion,* ed. J. Helm, 77–90. Seattle: University of Washington Press.

Kunitz, S. J. 1977. Underdevelopment and social services on the Navajo reservation. *Human Organization* 36:398–404.

Kunitz, S. J., J. E. Levy, and M. W. Everett. 1969. Alcohol cirrhosis among the Navajo. *Quarterly Journal of Studies on Alcohol* 30:672–85.

Kuttner, R. E., and A. B. Lorincz. 1967. Alcohol and addiction in urbanized Sioux Indians. *Mental Hygiene* 51:530–42.

———. 1970. Promiscuity and prostitution in urbanized American Indian communities. *Mental Hygiene* 54: 79–91.

Lang, G. C. 1979. Survival strategies of Chippewa drinkers in Minneapolis. *Central Issues in Anthropology* 1 (2): 19–40.

Larpenteur, C. 1962. *Forty years a fur trader on the upper Missouri: The personal narrative of Charles Larpenteur, 1833–1872,* ed. E. Coues. Minneapolis: Ross and Haines.

Lee, D. D. 1959. *Freedom and culture.* Englewood Cliffs, N.J.: Prentice-Hall.

Leland, J. 1976. *Firewater myths* (No. 11). New Brunswick, N.J.: Rutgers Center for Alcohol Studies, Publications Division.

———. 1977. North American Indian drinking and alcohol abuse: A critical review of the literature. Unpublished manuscript for inclusion in the NIAAA Third Special Report to Congress on Alcohol and Health. Rockville, Md.: National Clearinghouse for Alcohol Information.

———. 1978. Women and alcohol in an Indian settlement. *Medical Anthropology* 2 (4): 85–119.

———. 1979. The context of Native American drinking: What we know so far. In *Social drinking contexts, NIAAA research monograph no. 7*, eds. T. C. Harford and L. S. Gaines. Washington, D.C.: U.S. Government Printing Office.

———. 1980. Native American alcohol use: A review of the literature. In *Talapai to Tokay*, ed. P. D. Mails and D. R. McDonald, 1–56. New Haven, Conn.: HRAF Press.

Lemert, E. M. 1954. Alcohol and the Northwest Coast Indians. *University of California Publications in Culture and Society* 2 (6): 304–406.

———. 1956a. Alcoholism and the sociocultural situation. *Quarterly Journal of Studies on Alcohol* 17 (2): 306–17.

———. 1956b. On alcoholism among Northwest Coast Indians (Reply to Corder's review). *American Anthropologist* 58 (3): 561–62.

———. 1958. The use of alcohol in three Salish Indian tribes. *Quarterly Journal of Studies on Alcohol* 19 (1): 90–107.

———. 1967. *Human deviance, social problems and social control*. Englewood Cliffs, N.J.: Prentice-Hall.

Levy, J. E. 1965. Navajo suicide. *Human Organization 24*, 308–318. Reprinted in *The emergent Native Americans*, ed. D. E. Walker, 594–613. Boston: Little, Brown, 1972.

Levy, J. E., and S. J. Kunitz. 1969. Notes on some White Mountain Apache social pathologies. *Plateau* 42:11–19.

———. 1971a. Indian drinking: Problems of data collection and interpretation. In *Proceedings: First Annual Alcoholism Conference on NIAAA*, ed. M. Chafetz, 217–36. Washington, D.C.: National Institute of Alcohol Abuse and Alcoholism.

———. 1971b. Indian reservations, anomie and social pathologies. *Southwestern Journal of Anthropology* 27:97–128.

———. 1974. *Indian drinking: Navajo practices and Anglo-American theories*. New York: Wiley-Interscience.

Lewis, T. H. 1975. A syndrome of depression and mutism in Oglala Sioux. *American Journal of Psychology* 132:753–55.

Lindquist, G. E. E. 1923. *The red man in the United States: An intimate study of the social, economic, and religious life of the American Indian*. New York: George M. Doran.

Littman, G. 1970. Alcoholism, illness, and social pathology among American Indians in transition. *American Journal of Public Health* 60 (9): 1769–87.

Lurie, N. O. 1971. The world's oldest on-going protest demonstration: North American Indian drinking patterns. *Pacific Historical Review* 40 (3): 311–32.

———. 1972. Indian drinking patterns. *American Journal of Orthopsychiatry* 42 (4): 554.

MacAndrew, C., and R. B. Edgerton. 1969. *Drunken comportment: A social explanation*. Chicago: Aldine.

MacGregor, G. 1945. *Warriors without weapons*. Chicago: University of Chicago Press.

Mails, P. D., and D. R. McDonald. 1977. Native Americans and alcohol: A preliminary annotated bibliography. *Behavior Science Research* (3): 169–96.

———. 1980. *Talapai to Tokay: A bibliography of alcohol use and abuse among native Americans of North America*. New Haven, Conn.: HRAF Press.

Mails, T. E. 1978. *Sundancing at Rosebud and Pine Ridge*. Sioux Falls, S.Dak.: Augustana College Press.

———. 1979. *Fools Crow*. Garden City, N.Y.: Doubleday.

Mandelbaum, D. G. 1965. Alcohol and culture. *Current Anthropology* 6 (3): 281–93. Reprinted in *Beliefs, behaviors and alcoholic beverages*, ed. M. Marshall, 14–30. Ann Arbor: University of Michigan Press, 1979.

Marshall, M., ed. 1979. *Beliefs, behaviors and alcoholic beverages*. Ann Arbor: University of Michigan Press.

Maynard, E. 1968. Negative ethnic image among Oglala Sioux high school students. *Pine Ridge Research Bulletin* 6:18–25.

———. 1969. Drinking as part of an adjustment syndrome among the Oglala Sioux. *Pine Ridge Research Bulletin* 9:33–51.

———. 1974. The growing negative image of the anthropologist among American Indians. *Human Organization* 33:402–4.

Maynard, E., and G. Twiss. 1970. *That these people may live: Conditions among the Oglala Sioux on the Pine Ridge reservation* (DHEW Publication HSM 72-508). Washington, D.C.: U.S. Government Printing Office.

McClelland, D. C., W. N. David, R. Kalin, and E. Wanner. 1972. *The drinking man*. New York: Free Press.

Medicine, B. 1969. The changing Dakota family and the stresses therein. *Pine Ridge Research Bulletin* 9:1–20.

———. 1973. The Native Americans. In *The outsiders*, ed. D. Spiegel and P. K. Spiegel. San Francisco: Rinehart Press.

———. 1978. We talk of mental health. *Newsletter of National Center for American Indian and Alaskan Native Mental Health* 2:5. Portland, Oreg.: White Cloud Center.

———. 1979. Native American communication patterns: The case of the Lakota speakers. In *Handbook of transcultural communication*, ed. M. K. Asante, E. Newmark, and C. A. Blake, 383–91. Beverly Hills, Calif.: Sage.

———. 1980. Culture and the schools: The interaction of sex roles. In *The occupational and educational needs of Native American women*, 137–61. Washington, D.C.: National Institute of Education.

———. 1981. American Indian family: Cultural changes and adaptive strategies. *Journal of Ethnic Studies* 8:13–23.

———. 1983. *Review of minority-related research funded by ADAMHA, 1967–1981— American Indians and Alaska Natives.* Washington, D.C.: National Institute of Mental Health.

Milligan, E. A. 1976. *Dakota twilight: The Standing Rock Sioux, 1874–1890.* Hicksville, N.Y.: Exposition Press.

Mindell, C. F. 1967. Clinical aspects of the use of alcohol among the Oglala Sioux. Unpublished paper presented at the Rosebud Sioux Tribal Workshop on Alcohol.

———. 1968. Poverty, mental health and the Sioux. *Pine Ridge Research Bulletin* 6:26–34.

Mirsky, J. 1937. The Dakota. In *Cooperation and competition among primitive peoples,* ed. M. Mead, 382–427. New York: McGraw-Hill.

Mohatt, G. 1972. The sacred water: The quest for personal power through drinking among the Teton Sioux. In *The drinking man,* ed. D. C. McClelland, W. N. Davis, R. Kalin, and E. Wanner, 261–75. New York: Free Press.

Mulford, H., and D. Miller. 1960. Drinking in Iowa. *Quarterly Journal in Studies of Alcohol* 21:26–39.

Nagler, M. 1970. *Indian in the city: A study of the urbanization of Indians in Toronto.* Ottawa: Canadian Research Center for Anthropology, Saint Paul University.

Nelson, B. 1946. *Land of the Dakotahs.* Minneapolis: University of Minnesota Press.

Officer, J. E. 1971. The American Indian and federal policy. In *The American Indian in urban society,* ed. J. O. Waddell and O. M. Watson, 8–65. Boston: Little, Brown.

Oglesby, R. E. 1963. *Manual Lisa and the opening of the Missouri for trade.* Norman: University of Oklahoma Press.

O'Reilly, H. 1889. *Fifty years on the trail: The remarkable story of the life of John Y. Nelson.* New York: [s.n.].

Poole, D. C. 1881. *Among the Sioux of Dakota: Eighteen months experience as an Indian agent.* New York: Van Norstrand.

Powers, W. K. 1977. *Oglala religion.* Lincoln: University of Nebraska Press.

Prager, K. M. 1972. Alcoholism and the American Indian. *Harvard Medical Alumni Bulletin* 46:20–25.

Price, J. A. 1968. The migration and adaptation of American Indians to Los Angeles. *Human Organization* 27:168–75.

———. 1975. Applied analysis of North American Indian drinking patterns. *Human Organization* 34:17–26.

Provinse, J. H. 1937. The underlying sanctions of Plains Indian culture. In *Social anthropology of North American tribes,* ed. F. Eggan. Chicago: University of Chicago Press.

Ray, A. J. 1978. *Indians in the fur trade: Their role as trappers, hunters, middlemen.* Toronto: University of Toronto Press.

Reasons, C. 1972. Crime and the American Indian. In *Native Americans today: Sociological perspectives*, ed. H. M. Nahr, B. A. Chadwick, and R. C. Day, 319–26. New York: Harper & Row.

Riggs, S. R. 1851. *Grammar and dictionary of the Dakota language* (Smithsonian contribution to knowledge, vol. 4). Washington, D.C.: Smithsonian.

Robbins, R. H. 1973. Alcohol and the identity struggle: Some effects of economic change on interpersonal relations. *American Anthropologist* 75 (1): 99–122.

Rohner, R. P., and E. C. Rohner. 1970. *The Kwakiutl Indians of British Columbia.* New York: Holt, Rinehart and Winston.

Ryan, W. 1971. *Blaming the victim.* New York: Vintage Books.

Sadler, P. O. 1979. The "Crisis Cult" as a voluntary association: An interactional approach to Alcoholics Anonymous. In *Beliefs, behaviors and alcoholic beverages*, ed. M. Marshall, 388–94. Ann Arbor: University of Michigan Press.

Sage, R. B. 1860. *Wild scenes in Kansas and Nebraska, the Rocky Mountains, Oregon, California, New Mexico, Texas, and the Grand Prairies.* Philadelphia: Carey and Hart.

Saslow, H. L., and M. J. Harrover. 1968. Research on psychosocial adjustment of Indian youth. *American Journal of Psychiatry* 125:224–31.

Saum, L. O. 1965. *The fur trader and the Indian.* Seattle: University of Washington Press.

Schusky, E. L. 1975. *The forgotten Sioux.* Chicago: Nelson-Hall.

Seligman, M. E. P. 1975. *Helplessness: On depression, development, and death.* San Francisco: W. H. Freeman and Company.

Slater, A. D., and S. L. Albrecht. 1972. The extent and cost of excessive drinking among the Uintah-Ouray Indians. In *Native Americans today: Sociological perspectives*, ed. H. M Bahr, B. A. Chadwick, and R. C. Day, 358–67. New York: Harper & Row.

Snyder, C. R. 1978. *Alcohol and the Jews: A cultural study of drinking and sobriety.* Carbondale: Southern Illinois University Press.

Spicer, E. H. 1962. *Cycles of conquest.* Tucson: University of Arizona Press.

Spindler, G. E., and L. S. Spindler. 1957. American Indian personality types and their sociocultural roots. *Annals of the American Academy of Political and Social Science* 311:147–57.

———. 1978. Identity, militancy and cultural congruence: The Monominee and the Kainai. *Annals of the American Academy of Political and Social Science* 436:73–85.

Spradley, J. P. 1970. *You owe yourself a drunk: An ethnography of urban nomads.* Boston: Little, Brown.

Stack, C. B. 1974. *All our kin.* New York: Harper & Row.

Stein, G. C. 1974. A fearful drunkenness: The liquor trade to the Western Indians as seen by European travellers in America, 1800–1860. *Red River Valley Historical Review* (Summer): 109–121.

Stephens, R. C., and M. H. Agar. 1979. "Red tape–white tape"—Federal-Indian funding relationships. *Human Organization* 38:283–93.

Stewart, O. C. 1964. Questions regarding American Indian criminality. *Human Organization* 23:64–76.

Sunder, J. E. 1963. The decline of the fur trade on the upper Missouri, 1850–1865. In *The American west, an appraisal*, ed. R. G. Ferris. Santa Fe: Museum of New Mexico Press.

Topper, M. D. 1976. The cultural approach, verbal plans, and alcohol research. In *Cross cultural approaches to the study of alcohol*, ed. M. Everett, J. O. Waddell, and D. B. Heath, 379–402. The Hague, Netherlands: Mouton.

———. 1980. Drinking as an expression of status: Navajo male adolescents. In *Drinking behavior among Southwestern Indians: An anthropological perspective*, ed. J. O. Waddell and M. W. Everett, 103–47. Tucson: University of Arizona Press.

———. 1981. The drinker's story: An important but often forgotten source of data. In *Cultural factors in alcohol research and treatment of drinking problems*, ed. D. B. Heath, J. O. Waddell, and M. D. Topper, 73–86. *Journal of Studies on Alcohol*, supplement 9.

Trimble, J. E., and B. Medicine. 1976. Development of theoretical models and levels of interpretation. In *Anthropology and mental health*, ed. J. Westermeyer, 161–200. The Hague, Netherlands: Mouton.

Tyler, S. L. 1973. *A history of Indian policy*. Washington, D.C.: U.S. Government Printing Office.

Uecker, A. E., L. R. Boutilier, and E. H. Richardson. 1980. "Indianism" and the MMPI scores of men alcoholics. *Journal of Studies in Alcohol* 41:357–62.

Underhill, R. M. 1938. *Singing for power*. Berkeley: University of California Press.

———. 1946. *Papago Indian religion* (Columbia University contributions to anthropology vol. LLL). New York: Columbia University Press.

———. 1953. *Red man's America*. Chicago: University of Chicago Press.

U.S. Census of Populations. 1973. *American Indians* (Population Volume II). Washington, D.C.: U.S. Department of Commerce, Bureau of Census.

———. 1980. 1984. *American Indian areas and Alaskan Natives villages: 1980 supplemental report*. PC 80-S1-13. Washington, D.C.: U.S. Government Printing Office.

U.S. Commission on Civil Rights. 1974. *Indian Civil Rights Issues in Montana, North, and South Dakota: A report*. Washington, D.C.: Montana–North Dakota-South Dakota Joint Advisory Commission.

———. 1977. Hearings. *Federal Bureau of Investigation—Indian reservations: Police abuse*. Washington, D.C.: U.S. Government Printing Office.

Useem, R. H., and C. K. Eicher. 1970. Rosebud reservation economy. In *The modern Sioux*, ed. E. Nurge, 3–34. Lincoln: University of Nebraska Press.

Valentine, C. A. 1968. *Culture and poverty: A critique and counterproposals*. Chicago: University of Chicago Press.

Vestal, S. 1934. *Warpath: The true story of the fighting Sioux told in a biography of Chief White Bull*. Boston: Houghton Mifflin.

Waddell, J. O. 1971. "Drink friends": Social contexts of convivial drinking and drunkenness among Papago Indian in an urban setting. In *Proceedings of the First Annual Alcoholism Conference of NIAAA*, ed. M. Chafetz, 237–51. Washington, D.C.: National Institute on Alcohol Abuse and Alcoholism.

———. 1975. For individual power and social credit: The use of alcohol among Tucson Papagos. *Human Organization* 34:9–15.

———. 1976. The place of the cactus wine ritual in the Papago Indian ecosystem. In *In the realm of the extra human: Ideas and actions*, ed. A. Bharati, 213–28. The Hague: Mouton.

Waddell, J. O., and M. W. Everett. 1980. *Drinking behavior among Southwestern Indians.* Tucson: University of Arizona Press.

Waldram, J. B. 2004. *Revenge of the Windigo: The construction of the mind and mental health of North American aboriginal peoples.* Toronto: University of Toronto.

Wallace, A. F. C. 1956. Revitalization movements. *American Anthropologist* 58 (2): 264–81.

———. 1959. The institutionalization of cathartic and control strategies in Iroquois religious psychotherapy. In *Culture and mental health*, ed. M. K. Opler, 63–96. New York: MacMillan.

———. 1969. *The death and rebirth of the Seneca.* New York: Random House.

Washburn, W. E. 1971. *Red man's land—white man's law.* New York: Charles Scribner's Sons.

Wax, M. L. 1971. *Indian Americans: Unity and diversity.* Englewood Cliffs, N.J.: Prentice-Hall.

Weaver, T., and R. H. Gartell. 1974. The urban Indian: Man of two worlds. In *Indians of Arizona: A contemporary perspective*, ed. T. Weaver, 72–96. Tucson: University of Arizona Press.

Weibel-Orlando, J. C. 1985. Indians, ethnicity and alcohol—contrasting perceptions of the ethnic self and alcohol use. In *The American experience with alcohol*, ed. L. A. Bennett and G. M. Ames. New York: Plenum Publishing Corporation.

Weisner, T. S., J. C. Weibel-Orlando, and J. Long. 1984. "Serious drinking," "white man's drinking" and "teetotaling"—drinking levels and styles in an American Indian population. *Journal of Studies on Alcohol* 45 (3): 237–50.

Westermeyer, J. J. 1972. Options regarding alcohol use among the Chippewa. *American Journal of Orthopsychiatry* 42:398–403.

———. 1974. "The drunken Indian": Myths and realities. *Psychiatric Annals* 4 (11): 29–36.

White, R. A. 1970. The lower-class "culture of excitement" among contemporary Sioux. In *The modern Sioux*, ed. E. Nurge, 175–97. Lincoln: University of Nebraska Press.

Whiting, J. W. M., and I. L. Child. 1953. *Child training and personality.* New Haven, Conn.: Yale University Press.

Whittaker, J. O. 1961. *Alcohol and the Standing Rock Sioux tribe.* Fort Yates, N.Dak.: Commission on Alcohol Standing Rock Sioux Tribe.

————. 1962. Alcohol and the Standing Rock Sioux tribe, I: The pattern of drinking. *Quarterly Journal of Studies on Alcohol* 23:468–79.

————. 1963. Alcohol and the Standing Rock Sioux tribe, II: Psychodynamic and cultural factors in drinking. *Quarterly Journal of Studies on Alcohol* 24:80–90.

————. 1966. The problem of alcoholism among American reservation Indians. *Alcoholism* 2:141–46.

————. 1982. Alcohol and the Standing Rock Sioux tribe: A twenty year follow-up study. *Journal of Studies on Alcohol* 43: 191–200.

Winkler, A. M. 1968. Drinking on the American frontier. *Quarterly Journal of Studies on Alcohol* 29 (2): 413–45.

Index

About the Author

Beatrice Medicine was a teacher and anthropologist who taught at over thirty universities throughout the United States and Canada. She was descended from the Sihasapa and Minneconjou bands of the Lakota Nation. Medicine received her undergraduate degree from South Dakota State University, her master's degree in sociology and anthropology from Michigan State University, and her Ph.D. from the University of Wisconsin at Madison. Medicine received the Distinguished Service Award, now known as the Franz Boas Award for Exemplary Service to Anthropology, from the American Anthropological Association in 1991. In 1996 she received the Malinowski Award from the Society for Applied Anthropology, in recognition for a lifetime commitment to the application of the social sciences to contemporary issues. In 1998, she received an honorary doctorate in humanities from Michigan State University for her contributions to her field. Shortly before her death in December 2005, she received the George and Louise Spindler Award for Education in Anthropology from the American Anthropology Association.

Dr. Medicine was active in research and writing on the roles of Indian women, Lakota culture, gender, art, and acculturation studies and on changes facing American Indian culture and traditions. She opened a way of establishing a more realistic picture of the plurality and diversity of Native American life, past and present, from real and complex Native American perspectives.

In addition to her teaching role, Dr. Medicine was active in civic matters that affect the rights of children, women, ethnic minorities—especially American Indians (or, as they are known in Canada, Native or First

Beatrice Medicine in traditional dress at age 30, circa 1953. Photograph by James C. Garner.

Nations)—and gay/lesbian and transgendered individuals. She served as head of the Women's Branch of the Royal Commission on Aboriginal Peoples for the Canadian government, helping to draft legislation to further protect the legal rights of native families there.

Medicine was also actively involved in establishing American Indian Centers in Seattle, Vancouver, and Calgary and served as a consultant and advisor to numerous cities and other governmental entities on social issues, as well as public and private foundations nationwide. She served as an expert witness in several trials pertaining to the rights of American Indians, including the 1974 federal case brought against the individuals involved in the Wounded Knee takeover of 1973.

Issues of indigenous peoples across the world were of great interest to Medicine, and she traveled and lectured in Germany, Peru, Australia, New Zealand, Yugoslavia, Portugal, the Netherlands, Russia, Botswana, Italy, Switzerland, Lithuania, and Great Britain. Dr. Medicine was the author of

The Native American Woman: A Perspective and *Learning to Be an Anthropologist and Remaining "Native": Selected Writings* (edited with Sue-Ellen Jacobs). She coauthored *The Hidden Half: Studies of Plains Indian Women* with Patricia H. Albers, and produced a documentary video in 1997 on Eastern European "Indian hobbyists" with director Liucija Baskauskas entitled *Seeking the Spirit: Plains Indians in Russia*. She was also a published poet and fiction writer.